SIMONE WEIL
by Robert Coles

"Coles's biography is, in the end, a marvel of taking his subject seriously. . . . Perhaps the best way of putting his treatment is that it could not have appeared much earlier, since it is the result of many years of thinking through Weil's life and writings."

Eric O. Springsted, *Commonweal*

"The legendary Weil—part saint, part literary genius, part patriot, part mystic—holds a clear fascination for many, including Pulitzer-winner Coles. Indeed, the key to her psychic cache is hard to find, but Coles puts his special gifts to work in helping readers better understand this strange and tormented woman. . . .

"Weil was an intellectual who believed that one must put one's body on the line. In her case, the body was frail, but her will was indomitable. Coles's conversations with Anna Freud about this enigmatic figure are luminous points in a book already filled with passion and light."

Kirkus Reviews

"The life and thinking of Weil, a teacher and writer who died at 34 in 1943, offered Coles 'a chance to affirm an old love.' . . . Coles is one of the few American intellectuals who regard the spiritual life as an essential component to the political life. . . . With Simone Weil, whose 'The Need for Roots' and 'Waiting For God' are masterpieces, Coles is a passionate scholar. He scours the texts and letters of Weil's brief life and devotedly finds in them a record of uncommon intellectual honesty. . . . Throughout these well-crafted pages, Coles keeps his commentary grounded by referring to his work as a psychiatrist and teacher at Harvard."

Colman McCarthy, *The Washington Post*

"A new study of this brilliant, perplexing and 'unnerving' French thinker . . . is certainly called for and this perceptive one does her justice."

Publishers Weekly

"Recommended for all Weil collections."

Choice

"Coles's portrait of Simone Weil is . . . well researched and finely presented. The author spent nearly three decades investigating and discussing the brief, but intense life of one of France's most enigmatic personalities. . . . Like a shooting star interrupting the darkness of the night sky, she illuminated contemporary philosophy and all too quickly burned out. Fortunately, her legacy survives in her writings and through current attempts—like this excellent biography—to understand this multifaceted individual."

Pittsburgh Press

"Dr. Coles takes up certain themes and passions that preoccupied his subjects, and wrestles with them as one might do with those of any figure who has become a lifelong spiritual companion. . . . To Dr. Coles, irony and paradox are the very conditions of life, and in Weil he finds much to try to explain. Straight off he confronts her probable suicide and links it — successfully, I think, with her lifelong aspiration to the condition of hunger, not only as a way of sharing the deprivations of those who suffer, but as a spiritual condition of those who, as she puts it, are 'waiting for God'."

The New York Times Book Review

"It seems to me appropriate, if not inevitable, that Robert Coles would, at some point, write of Simone Weil and Dorothy Day.

"There is a word out of classical theology that sticks in the mind; 'connaturality.' Coles is a 'natural' to examine and illuminate such lives. I do not mean this in any superficial sense, rather in likeness of outlook, sense of vocation, what one might call style of soul.

"Very early in his medical career, Coles, through luck and friendship, discovered the domestic third world that coexists, barely, in our savage streets. He became the advocate of the voiceless, the healer of untouchables. He staked his credentials on this neglected work, so neatly sidestepped by classy colleagues. Meantime, he was constantly fueling his passion with the study of lives very like his own: Bernanos, Bloy, W. C. Williams, to name a few. And of course, Day and Weil."

Daniel Berrigan

Radcliffe
Biography Series

———

DOROTHY DAY
A Radical Devotion
Robert Coles

SIMONE WEIL
A Modern Pilgrimage
Robert Coles

MARGARET BOURKE-WHITE
A Biography
Vicki Goldberg

MARY CASSATT
Nancy Hale

THE THIRD ROSE
Gertrude Stein and Her World
John Malcolm Brinnin

MARGARET FULLER
From Transcendentalism to Revolution
Paula Blanchard

EMILY DICKINSON
Cynthia Griffin Wolff

CHARLOTTE MEW AND HER FRIENDS
Penelope Fitzgerald

THE ALCHEMY OF SURVIVAL
One Woman's Journey
John E. Mack, M.D.
with Rita S. Rogers, M.D.

———

BALM IN GILEAD
Journey of a Healer
Sara Lawrence Lightfoot

MARIA MONTESSORI
A Biography
Rita Kramer

A MIND OF HER OWN
The Life of Karen Horney
Susan Quinn

FORTHCOMING

WOMEN OF CRISIS
Lives of Struggle and Hope
Robert Coles and Jane Hallowell Coles

WOMEN OF CRISIS II
Lives of Work and Dreams
Robert Coles and Jane Hallowell Coles

PUBLISHED BY DELACORTE PRESS

HELEN AND TEACHER
The Story of Helen Keller and Anne Sullivan Macy
Joseph P. Lash

BUYING THE NIGHT FLIGHT
Georgie Anne Geyer

Radcliffe
Biography Series

Simone Weil

A Modern Pilgrimage

Robert Coles

A MERLOYD LAWRENCE BOOK

ADDISON-WESLEY PUBLISHING COMPANY, INC.
Reading, Massachusetts   Menlo Park, California
Don Mills, Ontario   Wokingham, England   Amsterdam   Bonn
Sydney   Singapore   Tokyo   Madrid   San Juan

———

Permissions appear on page 173.

Library of Congress Cataloging-in-Publication Data

Coles, Robert.
  Simone Weil, a modern pilgrimage.

  (Radcliffe biography series)
  "A Merloyd Lawrence book."
  Bibliography: p.
  Includes index.
    1. Weil, Simone, 1909–1943.   2. Philosophers – France –
Biography.   I. Title.   II. Series.
B2430.W474C65   1987   194   86-32292
  ISBN 0-201-02205-2
  ISBN 0-201-07964-X

Cover design by Copenhaver Cumpston
Text design by Douglass G. A. Scott
Calligraphy by Jean Evans
Set in 11-point Sabon by Neil W. Kelley, Georgetown, MA

ABCDEFGHIJ–HA–89

First printing, April 1987
First paperback printing, January 1989

The Radcliffe
Biography Series

Radcliffe College is pleased and proud to sponsor the Radcliffe Biography Series depicting the lives of extraordinary women.

Each volume of the series serves to remind us of two of the values of biographical writing. A fine biography is first of all a work of scholarship, grounded in the virtues of diligent and scrupulous research, judicious evaluation of information, and a fresh vision of the connections between persons, places, and events. Beyond this, fine biographies give us both a glimpse of ourselves and a reflection of the human spirit. Biography illuminates history, inspires by example, and fires the imagination to life's possibilities. Good biography can create lifelong models for us. Reading about other people's experiences encourages us to persist, to face hardship, and to feel less alone. Biography tells us about choice, the power of a personal vision, and the interdependence of human life.

The timeless women whose lives are portrayed in the Radcliffe Biography Series have been teachers, reformers, adventurers, writers, leaders, and scholars. The lives of some of them were hard pressed by poverty, cultural heritage, or physical handicap. Some of the women achieved fame; the victories and defeats of others have been unsung. We can learn from all of them something of ourselves. In sponsoring this series, Radcliffe College is responding to the continuing interest of our society in exploring and understanding the experience of women.

The Radcliffe Biography project found its inspiration in the publication in 1971 of *Notable American Women*, a scholarly encyclopedia sponsored by Radcliffe's Schlesinger Library on the history of women in America. We became convinced that some of the encyclopedia's essays should be expanded into full-length biographies, so that a wider audience could grasp the many contributions women have made to American life – an awareness of which is as yet by no means universal. Since then the concept of the series has expanded to include women of our own times and in other countries. As well as commissioning new biographies, we are also adding reprints of distinguished books already published, with introductions written for the series.

It seems appropriate that an institution dedicated to the higher education of women should sponsor such a project, to hold a mirror up to the lives of particular women, to pay tribute to them, and so to deepen our understanding of them and of ourselves.

We have been joined in this project by a remarkable group of writers. I am grateful to them and to the editorial board – particularly to Deane Lord, who first proposed the series, both in concept and in detail. Finally, I am happy to present this volume in the Radcliffe Biography Series.

> Matina S. Horner
> President

Radcliffe College
Cambridge, Massachusetts

———

To Jane,
once more, with love and with thanks
for all the wonderful years,
and with special thanks,
in connection with this project,
for the encouragement, the prodding, the tough criticism,
during those early morning breakfasts.

Contents

Preface

My first encounter with Simone Weil came in 1950, in a college course taught by the late Perry Miller, "Classics of the Christian Tradition." On that particular day (a Wednesday noon, I remember), Professor Miller was speaking about Pascal, as well as some French writers in this century who resemble Pascal in one way or another. Simone Weil stood out in this discussion, and he told us, with great enthusiasm, as much as he then knew about her. Little of her work had been published in the United States at that time, though in a couple of years G. P. Putnam would be offering *Waiting for God, The Need for Roots,* and *Gravity and Grace.* Professor Miller had learned of her ideas and her writing during the Second World War, and he had tracked down some of her essays. Not much had been published, even in French, yet her legend had been passed along from person to person, in Europe and then in the United States.

I heard of her again when I was in medical school, from Reinhold Niebuhr, who mentioned her, along with Dietrich Bonhoeffer, in a course at the Union Theological Seminary. I happened to attend the lecture when her name came up and was struck by Niebuhr's perplexity as he struggled with her obvious brilliance and what he saw as her serious blindspots and confusions. Next, after an interlude of a year's internship and a couple of years of psychiatric residency, I found myself studying child psychiatry and, for diver-

xv

sion, or maybe sanity's sake, taking a seminar with Paul Tillich at Harvard. He brought up Simone Weil and suggested that I read her work, learn what I could about her life, and write the paper required in his course on some aspect of her writing, or perhaps attempt a short biographical essay. Since I read French, I could get at some of her untranslated pieces. Besides, Tillich said, my "training would be of help in understanding her life."

The result was my first effort to approach this puzzling, unnerving figure. Her mix of political analysis, religious or moral reflection, and social inquiry – all rendered in a wonderfully lucid and compelling prose – seemed rare, suggestive, and inspiring. Tillich wrote a number of helpful comments on my paper, including a suggestion that I "pursue further" this "interest" of mine.

I wasn't sure at the time that I had such an interest! I certainly knew that other concerns had a stronger claim on my time and energy: the completion of child psychiatry training; the fulfillment of an obligation to the military under the old doctors' draft law; the personal experience of psychoanalysis, followed by learning its principles in seminars. Still, during those years, whenever I saw the name Simone Weil in print, I paid attention. Gradually I accumulated a rather substantial collection of her writing and of essays written about her. Several times I discussed her with my analyst who, fortunately, wasn't afraid to be interested in religion and religious writers. Those were comfortable, indeed memorable, conversations. He, too, encouraged me to try to figure out, as he once put it, "where she was saner than some, and when she was probably a little loony." A nice way, I still think, of regarding her.

The years passed, and as I began to write about my work in the South, the moral and religious side of the events I had witnessed became increasingly evident. Martin Luther King, Jr., Andrew Young, and other ministers my wife and I had come to know had been struggling not only with civil authorities, with politicians, and with all sorts of laws and customs, but with their own religious ideals, with their own moral values. They were also challenging a particular kind of Christianity. As I thought about them I suddenly found myself going back to Simone Weil, and talking about her, too, with the religious leaders and with young people, during the Mississippi Summer Project of 1964, launched by several hundred college students from all over the United States.[1] I also found myself mentioning her in what I was writing frequently enough to begin thinking I ought to stop, to try to understand the significance of her insights and values for so many of us today.

Since 1966 or so, I have kept reading her, struggling with conflicting feelings and opinions of her, and have done a fair amount of writing on one or another aspect of her thought, drawing on her many-sided political essays, her historical or literary pieces, letters, and journal entries. This writing took the form of articles, book reviews, a chapter in a book, an introduction to another book about her spiritual life,[2] and finally, what I thought would be a final effort, a more or less autobiographical piece in the *Yale Review*.[3] In this last essay, at the request of the editor, I tried to explain my continuing personal entanglement with this perplexing figure. I thought I was saying farewell – acknowledging respect, even devotion, but also frustration, irritation that could turn to a shudder of strong disapproval, and at times, to a clinician's pity. How could someone so wonderfully sensitive, thoughtful, and decent, someone whose words could be so free of cant, hypocrisy, and banality, someone who was brave both personally and intellectually, and honorable as well, *also* be so blind, so willfully obtuse, and, alas, so forbidding? What was one to make of certain aspects of Simone Weil's life and thought, which those who admire her make a point of not discussing at any great length or depth: her manner of death; her personality; her attitude toward the Old Testament, toward her own ancestors, the Jewish people; her response to Vichy France, to fascism as well as communism? I had alluded to these issues, as have others, but with too much restraint. Maybe I felt ashamed – for her and for myself as her largely unstinting admirer and sometime apologist.

But when I tried to lay these questions to rest, they would not go away. A remark once made by her brother, mathematician André Weil, kept coming back to me. At a public conference (there have been several) on her life and thought, he and I were scheduled to talk and answer questions together.[4] As I listened to him, I began to learn that one can hold someone high in one's mind and heart and still stop short of veneration, still keep one's critical wits about oneself and thereby, in the long run, do the admired figure a favor. "My sister did not spend her life analyzing idolatry," he said, "in order to end up becoming an idol." The remark was made wryly and not without affection. It is just this spirit of ironic affection that I have tried to keep in mind while making yet another attempt, in this book, to understand this most extraordinary woman.

A similar spirit pervaded the encouragement my wife offered throughout this task. What I say in the dedication is a mere beginning: it was she who tired, finally, of my alternately hot and cold reactions, she who kept telling me to get on with it, to delve into some of these troublesome matters, to take a chance at exploring them in a more extended manner — a chance to affirm an old love and take on a few genuine demons. Gratefully I say thanks to her.

I am much obliged to Merloyd Lawrence, who has had a long-standing interest in Simone Weil's ideas, for her patient but firm confidence that somehow, sometime, this book would be written — and for her attentive editorial work. I also warmly thank André Weil for our talks and exchanges, and Sissela Bok for help at a critical moment, through several wise letters. Over the years many students have read the Simone Weil essays and books I have assigned and have approached me after lectures, or come to my office hours, with their interest in and affection toward her ignited, their strong disapproval also in full sway. I am grateful to all of them, and especially to my former student and good friend Bruce Diker for his much-needed encouragement as I worked on the chapter "Her Jewishness," a hard one for me to write. "You can't read Simone Weil without getting really worked up," one freshman said to me, and that not especially elegant remark has turned out to be accurate. Simone Weil simply did not know how to live a bored life, and her writings rarely leave her readers — let alone her biographers — with a moment's indifference.

Finally, I acknowledge a great debt to Anna Freud, who during many conversations helped me think through the moral and psychological complexities that the life of Simone Weil presents to her readers. It was Miss Freud, actually, who first suggested that I try to take on some of those complexities in a book.[5] We both had read Simone Pétrement's biography and realized that a rerun was unnecessary. Our discussions about Simone Weil's life were very illuminating, and I have woven some of Miss Freud's remarks into this book.

The essays that follow are efforts to comprehend certain themes which Simone Weil herself kept approaching in the fifteen or so writing years of her life – a study of her central concerns, if not passions or obsessions. No matter my demurrers, I have embarked on this project out of great respect. At her best, Simone Weil was not only a brilliant and original social observer, political theorist, and moral philosopher, but an extraordinary pilgrim of the twentieth century. Her personal struggles, as rendered in her essays, her wonderfully dense yet lucid *pensées* – a series of journal entries – and her most wayward or extreme pronouncements address matters of particular concern to anyone in an industrial nation today. She was, as Anna Freud put it, "a marvelous scold." For many of us who try to figure out how to live our lives – what values and beliefs to uphold, what actions to pursue – her example, her achievements, her frustrations, her intellectual or moral or religious impasses, and her failures, self-described or apparent to us from hindsight, all can serve to focus the mind, enlarge the heart, and stir the soul.

Chronology

1909	Born February 3, in Paris, to Dr. Bernard and Selma Weil
1914	Dr. Weil mobilized into the French army soon after the outbreak of World War I. The family, including André, born 1906, moves each time he is transferred.
1916	Attends the Lycée Montaigne in Paris for three months
1917	Dr. Weil assigned to Laval, where Simone enters the girls' lycée
1919	Several months after the end of World War I, the family returns to Paris. In September, Simone enters the Lycée Fénelon.
1924	Admitted to the baccalauréat. Enters the Lycée Duruy.
1925	Passes her baccalauréat exams in philosophy
1925–28	Attends the Lycée Henri IV, where she studies with the philosopher Alain (Emile-Auguste Chartier)

1928   Passes the entrance examinations for the École
Normale Supérieure, in first place. Enters at the end
of the year.

1931   Receives her agrégation diploma and takes her first
teaching post at the girls' lycée in Le Puy.

1932   Engages in a demonstration for unemployed
workers. Transferred to the girls' lycée in Auxerre
by the school authorities.

1933   Appointed to the girls' lycée in Roanne. Participates
in a march of miners organized by the Confederated
Miners' Union, December 3. Meets Trotsky
December 31.

1934   Takes leave from teaching and works as a power
press operator at Alsthom Electrical Works in Paris.

1935   Takes job at the J. J. Carnaud et Forges de Basse
Indre factory in Billancourt, where she works at a
stamping press. In June works on a milling machine
at the Renault factory at Boulogne-Billancourt.

         Appointed to teach philosophy at the girls' lycée in
Bourges.

1936   In August, leaves to join the republican front in the
Spanish civil war. Joins an international group allied
with an anarchist trade union in Aragon. While on
bivouac a few weeks later, steps into a cooking pot
of boiling oil. Leaves the front and is treated in
Sitgès.

1937   On sick leave for the school year 1936–1937, visits Italy in the spring. In Assisi, in a chapel frequented by Saint Francis, feels compelled to kneel and pray. Teaches for the fall term at the girls' lycée in Saint-Quentin, a working-class town near Paris.

1938   Takes another sick leave in January. At Easter, attends services at the Benedictine abbey of Solesmes, where "the Passion of Christ entered my being once and for all."

1939   Six months' holiday with her family. When war is declared in September, they return to Paris. Reads the Bhagavad-Gita for the first time.

1940   After the Armistice, moves with her family to Vichy, then in October to Marseille, where she becomes involved with the literary magazine *Cahiers du Sud* and the group associated with it. Requests a new teaching post, but receives no reply from the minister of education, no doubt because of the Vichy anti-Jewish laws.

1941   Begins to study Sanskrit. Meets the Dominican priest Father J.-M. Perrin, who helps her find farm work with Gustave Thibon, a Catholic writer in the Ardèche.

1942   Leaves her notebooks with Thibon and sails to New York with her parents on May 17, after two weeks in a refugee camp in Casablanca. Eager to join the Resistance movement headquartered in London, she writes various officials there. Sails to Liverpool in November. Is held in a detention camp.

1943   Obtains work as a writer with the Free French or-
        ganization in London. Her reports for them include
        The Need for Roots. In April enters the hospital,
        where tuberculosis is diagnosed. Refuses food. Dies
        on August 24. Buried in Ashford, Kent.

Simone Weil

I cannot conceive the necessity for God to love me, when I feel so clearly that even with human beings affection for me can only be a mistake. But I can easily imagine that he loves that perspective of creation which can only be seen from the point where I am. But I act as a screen. I must withdraw so that he may see it.

To see a landscape as it is when I am not there . . .

It is necessary to uproot oneself. To cut down the tree and make of it a cross, and then to carry it every day.

Gravity and Grace

Introduction
to a Life

It is hard to believe that anyone in the world who knew Simone Weil in 1943, the year she died, could have imagined the degree of sustained attention, even reverence, she would receive in the following years. Thirty-four years old, she lay dying of tuberculosis in a sanitarium outside London. There she had spent the sad last days of her lonely, inconspicuous life. It was a bleak year – for London, for England, for the entire Western world: Hitler dominated Europe, apparently an enduring threat to every human being on the planet. Anna Freud, who lived in England then and was also a refugee from the Continent (she from Austria, Simone Weil from France), described the summer of 1943 in this manner:

"I know from memory, as well as from notes of mine and letters
I received and answered, what a dark year that was. The war
seemed endless; so many innocent people were being killed in
the blitz, the bombings that kept being visited on us. Everywhere Hitler's armies were still on the offensive. We dreamed
of a turn-around, but it *was* a dream. The reality was grim. It
took a special person to be hopeful that year." [1]

At that time and place, to be seriously ill at such a young age was not as noteworthy as it might be now: every day babies and young children were being killed during air raids or in Nazi death camps scattered over several nations. Yet to her family and the handful of people who knew Simone Weil well and appreciated her utterly unique gifts, her last illness was additional evidence of the extreme jeopardy fate had visited upon civilization itself. Simone Weil was an exceptionally brilliant scholar whose interests were eminently those of high European culture: a classical education which kept easy, relaxed company with a thorough, assured knowledge of mathematics, physics, biology – the full range of natural science.

We will never know her sense of herself at the end of her life – her sense, that is, of her significance to her country, to her colleagues and friends, scattered across France, the United States, and England. We do know, from her own words, how fiercely Simone Weil was combating the conventional life, the concerns most of us share: that our bodies be well fed and tended; that we find love, hold on to the love of others – our husbands, our wives, our children, our friends; that our work be as useful and rewarding as possible; that we feel a part of a particular community, a particular world. She never let herself fall into the commonplace, the routines of millions of lives, Catholic or Protestant or Jewish: people waking up and feeling hunger and eagerly subduing it with a hearty breakfast; people making love; people proudly trying to do their work, and if successful, glad for themselves, for those with whom they can share the rewards; people who want to stay here and enjoy this life, for all its injustice and tragedy and mystery, and see it continued in others, in children and grandchildren, in students or patients or clients or just plain strangers, in the human parade.

No wonder, then, that a shudder rises when we contemplate the life of Simone Weil. Even as a child she couldn't just eat; she worried about those who didn't or couldn't by virtue of their economic circumstances.[2] Nor could she let her body enjoy or be enjoyed by others. She made herself, in many respects, an "untouchable" – a hard conclusion to draw as one sifts through pictures of her when she was an adolescent, with friends and family, skiing, smiling, lovely to look at, vital in appearance and manner. Her

4

young life apparently was ready to reach outward, as others, gifted and attractive, reached toward her.

But her stringent, articulate mind would not allow her to find company, let alone recognition and devotion. Simone Weil was forever on the move, morally and spiritually and politically and culturally, so that, by the time Hitler forced her and her family into exile, she was already chronically displaced. In the end, she was by all human standards utterly alone, and yet – here is the mystery – perhaps quite fulfilled: an expectant soul whose time of encounter with God had at last arrived.

Her pilgrimage ended on Tuesday, August 24, 1943. Seriously ill with tuberculosis, Simone Weil had been taken to the Grosvenor Sanatorium at Ashford in Kent, where, refusing to cooperate with the staff's efforts to treat her, she died. Her doctors felt she had hastened, if not caused, her own death. She was buried in the Ashford New Cemetery, in grave number 79. The world went on its murderous way – though, as Anna Freud reminded me when we talked about Simone Weil's last weeks, "even during the worst times, in London people found their small pleasures in life." Her remark seemed to emphasize Simone Weil's isolation at the last – a strange and stubborn hospital patient who seemed eager for her last breath.

But Simone Weil was not always beyond anyone's comprehension or the victim of bad luck and a discouraging life. She was born on February 3, 1909, in Paris, the second child and only daughter of Bernard Weil, a well-known, successful physician, and Selma (Reinherz) Weil. Both parents were Jewish. Her paternal grandmother, who was Orthodox, kept a kosher house. Her maternal grandparents were Russian Jews (her mother was born in Rostov-on-Don) who had moved westward. Her mother's father, Adolphe Reinherz (Simone was given the middle name Adolphine in his honor), was a successful businessman who wrote poetry in Hebrew and amassed a substantial Hebrew library. Simone's older and only brother, André, was born in May 1906, and at this writing is in his eighty-first year, a retired member of the distinguished scientific cardre at the Institute for Advanced Study in

Princeton, New Jersey. His field is mathematics, and he is known throughout the world as an important and erudite thinker. Before Simone Weil died, her brother had come to America, married, and fathered a daughter. The brother and the niece figure in her letters, in her struggles to decide what is right and wrong – for example, to be baptized or not.

It is interesting that this brilliant girl had an older brother just as brilliant – indeed, even more brilliant in the conventional scientific tradition valued so highly by the Weil family, whose values were thoroughly secular. André, a child prodigy, was a mathematician of the greatest talent, even as a youngster. Simone mentioned in her writing her envy of her brother and her awareness, while she was still young, of his budding genius. Since she, too, was precociously sensitive and aware, a young mind able to worry about France's situation in the First World War, as Simone Pétrement tells us, she was no doubt able to take stock of her own situation. In the shadow of the slightly older boy for whom the world seemed to be waiting eagerly, she may have wondered about her own destiny. What awaited her – a girl growing up early in this century in a bourgeois French milieu?

In trying to understand the life of someone whom doctors declared a young suicide, a psychiatrist finds it all too tempting to scrutinize her childhood, especially when she had no later family life – she never married or had children – and especially, too, when she herself made references to her family that sound a note of pain. When I discussed Simone Weil's childhood with Anna Freud, and showed her the letters Simone had written to her parents and her brother, and the family pictures of the Weil children, she reminded me that

"pictures don't tell everything, nor do diary entries or letters. But from all I've read, the family seems to have been solid and strongly connected, I suppose too much so for the daughter's long-range good – the intense attachment to the mother, and vice versa. But I don't think a clinical emphasis is justified here – not on the basis of what you and I can surmise after reading those letters and looking at the pictures. Of course, when we hear about what started happening to her in adolescence – the very painful migraines – and when we learn what happened to her later in life – how it ended – we are going to return to her childhood in our minds and maybe find reasons to be concerned. But we should admit to ourselves that we are glancing back ex post facto . . . You and I have known some extremely unhappy families whose children seem headed for the most serious of difficulties, yet, later in life, those children seem to have come through just fine."

Anna Freud then went on to point out the extraordinary brilliance of those two children.

"These were not just a pair of bright children from a comfortable and intelligent family. They both seem to have been truly exceptional from the beginning, and *both* seem to have become successful, extremely successful. André Weil is one of the world's leading mathematicians; and here you and I are poring over the words and ideas of Simone Weil. And not just us alone! The whole [intellectual] world knows of *her*."

Miss Freud's words sent me back to contemplate the mystery of those two lives – of any lives – not quite the "mystery" Simone Weil embraced so eagerly, but a step in that direction. This sense of wonder puts the occasional psychological comment in perspective, a reminder that such a comment may still prove as elusive to definitive exploration as Miss Freud surmised.

Simone Weil was born at the end of a decade during which France was virtually split in two by the Dreyfus case, by anti-Semitism and its strong roots in that nation's bourgeoisie. When she was six, war broke out and her father was called to the army immediately. Her mother, with the two children, followed him all over France's western front, hence her unsettled home and school life. When Simone went to Spain in the civil war her parents were quick to follow; they were constantly at her side all her life, until the last months, when she left New York and crossed the Atlantic to enlist with the Free French in London. By then she had also, as we shall see, parted company with them in another way, with respect to the Old Testament, Judaism, her Jewish background.

Despite the early years of travel, war, and studying through correspondence, at the age of eight she was enrolled in the girls' lycée in Laval and at ten in the Lycée Fénelon in Paris. By fifteen she was studying the classics intensively and learning philosophy at the Lycée Victor Duruy, and by sixteen she was already a student, at the Lycée Henri IV, of the distinguished philosopher Alain, a pen name of Emile-Auguste Chartier. At only nineteen she had passed the entrance examination of the prestigious École Normale Supérieure; it is a well-known fact that she scored highest on that examination, and that the second highest score was received by a student also named Simone – last name: de Beauvoir. It was there, as a student, that Simone Weil started becoming the political person she would be for the remaining decade and a half of her life. She read Marx and came to admire his historical, social, and economic insights, but also to take issue with him. Her objections were not on any religious grounds – that would come later – but out of an early, feisty independence and a shrewd and logical mind that prompted her to ask questions, constantly, of those, dead or alive, whose words she found interesting and suggestive. She also declared herself to be a pacifist – she would repent on that score only with Hitler's rise, specifically, around the time of Munich; and she allied herself, enthusiastically, vocally, and with great dedication of street energy, to the cause of France's unions, the working class, and the poor. In France, as elsewhere, large numbers of people were barely surviving the Great Depression of the 1930s, which for a few years seemed on the verge of becoming a permanent condition for the Western capitalist nations.

By the age of twenty-one, Simone Weil had finished her thesis, titled "Science and Perception in Descartes," had passed her finals, and graduated. In the fall of 1931 she began her first job, as a philosophy instructor in the girls' lycée at Le Puy, seventy miles to the south and west of Lyons. While there she allied herself with the unemployed of the city and led a demonstration before the city council. This caused an enormous uproar, during which a conservative newspaper referred to Simone as a "red virgin of the tribe of Levi, bearer of Muscovite gospels." Despite petitions by her students and their parents, she was transferred to Auxerre, near Paris, also at a girls' lycée, but was soon dismissed, because she refused to teach the girls the rote learning the school expected. She wanted to stimulate thought, stir the imaginations of her pupils, and prompt their love for her classical passions. By 1933 she was back in the Lyons area, at Roanne, west of the city, once more at a girls' lycée. Once again, it was not only her teaching that caused her trouble; she was considered a dangerous leftist, a reputation further enhanced by her participation in the March of the Miners, a large-scale protest in Saint-Étienne against unemployment and a reduction in the miners' wages.

In 1934 she was relentlessly pushing herself with questions, the gist of which might be put this way: You are twenty-five, and you have strong intellectual interests, but you are also drawn to the world, moved by moral forces within you that have already given you trouble, so what do you plan to do? Move from lycée to lycée, in hopes of finding a situation in which you will be tolerated, even given sanction, rather than regarded as a radical, an anarchist, a danger to the young girls you are teaching? Return to the university, study further, become an avowed intellectual, write some articles and books, have an occasional go at politics, in the sense that petitions get signed, sides are taken, but as extracurricular activities? Quit teaching altogether and join a political group – become a full-time activist, a pamphleteer, whatever you can manage to do for the cause?

She chose none of those. Instead she applied for a leave to pursue her personal studies, but her studies were hardly abstract, theoretical, or academic. In December of 1934 she took a job as a power press operator at the Alsthom Electrical Works in Paris. She stayed there for four months, despite severe migraine that pressed upon her for days at a stretch and a chronic, painful sinusitis. She stayed there in order to see firsthand how it is, all the time, for working-class people. She stayed there, too, in a spirit of solidarity, of communion with others, an attempt not only to do a documentary field study, it might be called, but to put her body on the line. She had already become, in her early twenties, a stern critic of intellectuals, an unrelentingly harsh critic of what she regarded as their privileged and arrogant ways. She wanted an escape from libraries and salons and polite, speculative conversation, even though her mind was always busy with ideas and questions, with ruminations and objections to what she had read or heard, with proposals and alternatives.

No doubt some of her friends or acquaintances considered such a choice self-indulgent, quixotic, melodramatic, and moralistically self-serving, if not evidence of instability. (Several schools had, by then, no doubt reached similar conclusions.) Simone Weil herself may well have ached to be done with such work, a not very productive outlet for her many gifts. But she was convinced that hard physical work was essential for an intellectual, lest the mind become all too taken with itself, all too removed from the concrete realities of everyday life, the burdens that rest upon the overwhelming majority of the earth's population. To comprehend such lives with even reasonable accuracy, she believed, it is necessary to join their labor, at least for a time.

Whether this effort was silly romanticism or self-righteousness masked as idealism or a decent person's hard struggle to find out how to live and work in a morally useful way, and by so doing, to learn something precious, she persisted for over a year. In April of 1935 she was working as a packer in another factory, and in June of that year she was hired to operate a milling machine at the famous Renault works. At the end of the summer, however, she was so worn out that her parents had to intervene, taking her on holiday to Portugal. I believe it was then, in the autumn of 1935, that she began to look upward, so to speak. Her gaze, heretofore, had been directed laterally at her fellow intellectuals, and downward at the poor, the oppressed. (A moralist with Marxist inclinations, she had regarded the employers of these oppressed as even further "down.") In Portugal, after watching a procession of fishermen at the festival of their patron saint, she began to think about the role of Christianity in the lives of the poor, and in her own.

She had tried to take on her own class, the intelligentsia, by working in factories – an ethical statement on her part. This was the 1930s, and French capitalism, like American and English capitalism, had not yet come to terms with the unions, with the political and economic fight they were waging on behalf of a reasonable life for millions – a minimum wage, provisions for the elderly, health insurance, unemployment benefits, not to mention the elementary right to organize, to enter the political arena with some collective strength. Simone Weil's first impressions of working life confirmed her earlier, intellectual impressions of a proletariat badly abused. But in Portugal Simone Weil began to think somewhat differently. Her heart went out to the poor in those villages, where poverty was more wretched, by far, than in Paris: by all statistical measures, the families were much more vulnerable socially, economically, and medically. Yet something at work in her caused her to take a second look at them and at poverty, to move beyond the abstract, as she had tried to do while working on the assembly line. Now, while she was troubled by the sight of those living in needy circumstances, as she always would be, she was also inspired by certain virtues she couldn't help noticing.

As I will try to indicate in more detail, she had stumbled into an experience familiar in the history of social observation among intellectuals who have wanted to see firsthand how others live and share their fate for ethical as well as documentary purposes.[3] On the one hand, there is the anticipated scene of people down on their luck: children sick, parents without work or barely able to feed their families, schooling thoroughly inadequate, if at all available, abysmal sanitation – a sad litany known to public health doctors and nurses, muckraking journalists, and welfare workers. And yet, in our ghettos today or in those Portuguese villages, an outsider willing to stop and look and listen (and remove firmly any ideological glasses he or she happens to be wearing) will soon enough become confounded by something else waiting there to be noticed: people down and out, true, but capable, some of them, of thoughtfulness, perseverance, and an impressive kind of stoic forbearance. Sometimes those same people will show a personal honor, a courtesy and civility, a hospitality that make one go back home and take another look *there*, at one's neighbors, oneself. How does one comprehend *them*, in all their vanity, their conceits and deceits?

It was her great virtue that Simone Weil never turned away from such a dilemma. She was too smart and tough to romanticize the poor as individuals, or poverty as a condition. She was also too observant and honest to sweep the dilemma under the rug and keep reciting the same old formulaic banalities. Instead, she bowed to fate in all its ironic, paradoxical, inconsistent, and ambiguous nature, as her ancient Greek soul mates did: those who have nothing materially can have a moral or spiritual strength, whereas those who seem to have everything that the world has to offer in the way of possessions and power can be moral idiots, or maybe morally adrift and hungry, they know not for what.

As she contemplated such difficult matters – the various struggles people must wage, the victories that turn sour and the defeats that bring their own high-principled moments – she began to dwell on the teachings of Jesus and their many puzzles and riddles. Jesus kept company with people Simone Weil would call slaves, and saw them to be not quite as desperate as some of the high and mighty. In those Portuguese villages Jesus would have walked in comfort and joy: His people. Simone Weil began to realize that among the Parisian powerful He would be "rebuked and scorned," as He was twenty centuries ago – lowly, not fit for the elegance of the boss-world. The more she realized this, the more fully she understood the link between the simple faith of the Portuguese peasants and the message of the God they worshiped so earnestly, persistently, almost crazily, by the standards of the well-educated and well-off world to which she belonged.

In early 1936 she was eager to live among France's peasantry, to learn not only about their lives, but the secret of their daily courage, resourcefulness, and endurance. She sought what James Agee saw at work in rural Alabama and what prompted in him a revival of his lyrical religious sensibility. Simone Weil worked on a farm with great enthusiasm, but she also kept her eye on the rapidly deteriorating European political scene. What would happen, she wondered, to the farmers and factory workers if Hitler and Mussolini and the French Fascists and Stalin, with his murderous forced collectivization, took over more and more territory? In July of 1936 the Spanish civil war started, and rather quickly she was on a train for Barcelona, to do what she could for the republican, the Loyalist side. She went to Aragon, near Saragossa, and like George Orwell later, prepared to fight on the side of the anarchist forces. But she would be in Spain only a couple of months. While on bivouac along the Ebro River, she stepped into a pot of oil being heated to cook dinner, and she had to be hospitalized and returned to France. As her biographer Simone Pétrement has pointed out, her clumsiness probably saved her life, since the rest of her group was killed soon afterward.

In 1937 and 1938, her health got worse. Her headaches were exhausting, painful, nearly incapacitating. She traveled in early 1937 – Milan and Florence, Rome, and finally, Assisi. On a spring day in a chapel there, the very place where Saint Francis himself prayed, she got down on her knees, feeling God's pull. She tried a return to teaching in the fall of 1937, but couldn't manage the daily tasks, so fragile was her health. In essence she was under the care of her parents – able to read, write, meditate, think through her various points of view, but not go forth and manage an independent life.

At Easter 1938 she visited the Benedictine abbey at Solesmes, where she heard the Gregorian plainsong and reported a mystical experience: the Lord visiting her, summoning her. During this time a young Englishman introduced her to seventeenth-century English metaphysical poets, especially George Herbert and John Donne. She went to Italy for a month or so, in the summer. She was, by now, a religiously intense person, eager to consider the historical development of Christianity, its contemporary situation. One gathers that her parents offered no great opposition to this turn in her life. Not that she was interested in a conversion to Catholicism. In fact, as we shall see, her religious life was as unconventional and idiosyncratic as she herself. She was a solitary seeker of God's company, a mystic, not at all inclined to embrace the regular rhythms of an established church. She had a unique capacity to keep thinking politically, historically, and economically, at the same time embracing theology and religious philosophy. Moreover, her interests reached outside of Christianity. In 1939, as war began to ravage Europe, she was learning Sanskrit, reading the Bhagavad-Gita.

With a declaration of war against Germany by Premier Édouard Daladier in early September of 1939, the Weils, who had been staying in Geneva, hastened home. Hitler had marched into Poland in a surprise assault on September 1, the first of many such blitz-kriegs. At the time, for many religious and secular people alike of countries such as France and England, everything seemed in utter jeopardy. The Nazis were already showing a gangster mentality that made the First World War seem almost quaint and decorous by comparison. We laugh at the melodrama of *Casablanca* – Bogart and Bergman in their melancholy Paris fling, with the Wehrmacht soon enough coming around the corner to terminate not only their time together, but (the movie tells us through Bogart's pontifical and sentimental lines) civilization itself: the Dark Ages had arrived. Yet that was precisely what had happened – the apparent beginning of the end for the children of light, with the children of darkness seemingly invincible. Nor did the imminent threat of a "Dark Age" fail to register upon ordinary individuals, resonate in such a way that their everyday lives showed the toll, the frantic worry, the despair, and the heightened activity, the excitement that a war generates in people.

"I remember those days all too clearly," Anna Freud once told me.

"My father was dying that September, and the two events merged in our minds – England going to war, and France, and his coming death; it was as if the end of so much was happening all at the same time! Our patients – children or adults – kept struggling with their private difficulties, as we all do, no matter

the larger tragedies taking place in the world – but a war like
that war seemed catastrophic to almost everyone, even those
whose [self-] preoccupations might have offered them a degree
of protection! And for those who were politically aware and
sensitive to suffering, this was the worst possible event – a
tragedy that had devastating psychological consequences for
many very thoughtful people. *They knew* – knew what the
stakes were, how close to the worst kind of barbarism we'd
come! They were terribly alarmed, frightened."[4]

Among these was Simone Weil, though she, too, gathered energy
from the war, found a focus for her moral and imaginative gifts.
She abandoned her pacifism. In early 1940, months before the
Nazis marched through Holland, Belgium, and with astounding
speed, France itself, she had contrived her "Memorandum on the
Formation of a Front-Line Nursing Squad," in the hope that she
and others could be at the side of France's soldiers as they fought
the Nazi troops. It was, I suppose, as wildly impractical as many
of her other ideas, suggestions, and actions. She wanted, at one
or another time, intellectuals on the assembly lines of factories, or
on farms doing planting and harvesting. When the Spanish civil
war broke out, she wanted people like herself (she had absolutely
no training as a soldier or a nurse) fighting for the Loyalist government. After France's fall, she wanted to be parachuted, with others,
behind the German lines, so she might be of help to Resistance
fighters. What help did she imagine offering, given her chronic
medical problems even before she contracted the tuberculosis which
would completely undo her health, and in less than a year, take
her life? None, those she petitioned in the French government of
1940 quickly decided. As the Nazis approached Paris the Weils
fled, first to Vichy, then to Marseille. There Simone Weil continued
her intense social reflection and her religious contemplation. Her
notebooks grew. Her mind stretched itself further. She became
interested in the connections between ancient Greek and Christian
thought. She probed the mystical tradition, such as the writing of
John of the Cross.[5] She meditated with great devotion, prayed

repeatedly, and struggled with herself and others as to whether she ought to be baptized in the Catholic Church.

It was in Marseille that she took up with a group of social and religious idealists, men and women still reeling from the collapse of their country's war effort and already wondering (an act of faith?) what would happen, what ought to happen, after the dark days of the war were over. It was in Marseille that she learned she could no longer teach school – not that for some time she had been able to last the full school year – because she was Jewish. Her disturbing reply to the edict is discussed in Chapter 3 of this book. It was in Marseille that she attended meetings of the Young Christian Workers' Movement, a group that tried to connect a social and political reform with a Christian emphasis on reconciliation of those who had become secular antagonists. It was in Marseille, too, that she met two men who came to mean a lot to her, the priest Reverend Father J.-M. Perrin, a Dominican, and Gustave Thibon, a friend of his. Thibon gave her the work she so much wished to have: grape harvesting on his farm in September and October of 1941. During this time she continued her studies of Greek and Hindu philosophy, borrowing some books from the writer René Daumal, author of *Mont Analogue*, whom she had known as a student.

On May 17, 1942, she left France – for good, it would turn out. The Weils sailed on the S.S. *Maréchal Lyautey* for Morocco. Before she left she had entrusted her notebooks to Thibon, who would later arrange them into the volume *Gravity and Grace*. She had also visited a Benedictine abbey, and concluded in her mind that she was not going to live much longer, even though she had no evidence, then, of any life-threatening illness, and was only thirty-two years old. In Morocco – in Casablanca, as a matter of fact – this cultured and compassionate family had to stay over two weeks in a refugee camp, where they had to undergo hostile inquiry in crowded and unpleasant conditions – all the miseries of emigration enforced by the fear of another kind of journey: the train to one of the Nazi camps eastward, whence almost no one ever returned.

On July 8, 1942, after a month's crossing on the steamship *Serpa Pinto*, the Weils arrived in New York City. They leased an apartment on the sixth floor at 549 Riverside Drive, where they tried to breathe easier, relax, and enjoy their exceedingly good and relatively rare luck: safety in America. Maybe the parents could do so, but their daughter emphatically refused that privilege. She was absolutely determined to get back to Europe, to reach London, and to press upon the government of General Charles de Gaulle her scheme for behind-the-lines work with the Resistance in France.

Meanwhile, in Manhattan, she was still Simone Weil. As I will discuss later, her mind ventured constantly, hungrily from the safety and comfort of a Riverside Drive apartment to others living under far less fortunate conditions. She wanted to go South, to talk with black farm workers. She wanted to visit Harlem. She asked incessantly about who lives where in America, though one gathers she developed no great affection for the country. She went to Mass every day at a Catholic church on 121st Street in Manhattan, while keeping up her crusade to join the French Resistance. Her contacts in London, after a while, must have taken comfort in the fact that she was living in America during the summer and early fall of 1942.

Her determination to get to England, and thence to the Continent, was formidable. Simone Weil was prepared to risk a submarine-infested Atlantic, cross the ocean in the middle of a fierce naval war, and not least, leave her parents in the most decisive way imaginable. In saying farewell before the crossing from Marseille she had pointed out to a friend that the ocean would make a beautiful baptismal font. On November 9 she had her way: she boarded the Swedish ship *Valaaren*, headed for Liverpool – a long and far from luxurious voyage. Frail to begin with, she was even more wan and exhausted on her arrival. Because she had been enrolled in the Spanish republican cause, and had once been a pacifist, she was detained in a camp for two weeks after her arrival.

By Christmas of 1942, her last one on this earth, she was in London. She sought work with the Free French, and found a small group of friends. During the months that followed she worked with tremendous commitment of time and energy on her social and political vision of what postwar France ought strive to accomplish for its people. This writing would eventually become *The Need for Roots*. As she applied her mind to the future, however, her body began to weaken even further. By mid April she had to enter a London hospital, but once there she became a difficult, and eventually an impossible patient. She was diagnosed as tuberculous. At that time the only treatment available was complete bed rest and lots of good food. (Antibiotics were not widely used until later.) She would have no part of the treatment, however. Even before the doctors had given their advice, she had been restricting her food intake severely, missing meals, not eating all that was served her. She told some people that she wanted to eat no more than the ordinary French people under Nazi occupation were eating. She told others that she simply had no appetite and was working too hard even to think of food. The whole issue of food and the imagery of hunger in her writing is discussed in the following chapter.

Patients with tuberculosis, back then, often survived, if they followed a prescribed medical regimen and were lucky enough not to have the most serious form of the disease.[6] But Simone Weil seemed to have no interest in survival, at least the human survival most of us want. A discussion continues among many who knew or admire her as to whether she did or did not take her own life, whether she was anorectic, a masochist, irrational, or psychotic at the end of her life. Her doctors were confused, frustrated, and enraged by her behavior. Here was a young woman as bright as any human being could want to be, educated and refined, not poor or without friends, who yet had no interest in cooperating with her doctors and nurses. Ultimately they tried tube feeding in a futile effort to save her. She died alone, on August 24, a thirty-four-year-old woman mourned by only a handful of London friends.

At the time of her death, she had earned no awards that made her famous, no honors, prizes, or distinctions of any public kind. She'd gone from school to school in a dismal teaching career. She had published no books and only a handful of articles, and these in obscure periodicals – radical ones at that. She had been the subject of no articles, essays, or biographies. She had a small family who would miss her terribly, and a handful of devoted friends who would be similarly grief stricken. Her ideas impressed few of those around her as practical or useful. Perhaps some of the Free French who did get to know her and read her proposals were inclined to the view held by her doctors, that she was not quite right in her head, a difficult person with peculiar ideas, both grandiose and cranky.

After the war was over, friends who had read her manuscripts, letters, and notebooks began to think of what they ought do with them – with their memory, as well, of someone whose mind and heart and soul, they believed, were truly exceptional. The result, over a span of a decade or so, was the publication of her writing as articles and books in her native France, and, gradually, their translation into other languages. Soon a number of prominent writers – philosophers, novelists, poets, political essayists, and theologians – began to mention her and this or that idea she had proposed. She was passed from person to person, and then to the public at large, through an increasing number of articles devoted to her thinking, her manner of living, her haunting, unnerving life. Later, full-fledged biographical studies appeared, along with exegetical attempts to fathom her thought, which was hardly meant to be systematic, or a definitive statement. She was, after all, so young, and trying so hard to figure out for herself what to think, what to believe, how to spend her time on this earth.

One does best, then, to accept her writing for what it was, a gift of the gods who resided in her, inspired sparks that had not yet come together as a single flame. She has now become an extremely important figure among the Western intelligentsia, and were she alive, she might face her audience with a wry smile, maybe an expression of shame or regret, perhaps a fiery anger and scorn. In any event, she was an intellectual who might have fought many more battles, won many wars, and achieved during her lifetime a measure of universal respect. She was an awesome presence to many who knew her. Had she lived, her ascetic, disciplined, ever provocative intellect, tempered by a soul growing larger and stronger, might have led its own legion of slaves, even as she claimed to be one forever.

On the other hand, there was a side of her that has deeply troubled some who have taken the time and energy to try to know her well. As I was finishing this book, I read a letter Dietrich Bonhoeffer wrote to his fiancée, Maria von Wedermeyer.[7] Ironically, the letter was written on August 12, 1943, just a few days before Simone Weil died. Bonhoeffer, the German aristocrat and brilliant theologian, who dared fight the Nazis with all his might, was then confined to a concentration camp. Like Simone Weil, he had left the safety of America in 1939 to cross the Atlantic and take up personal arms against what he regarded as the worst of all evils. He was killed by the Nazis in April 1945, also still in his thirties. But dark as the world was in 1943 for Bonhoeffer, too, he wrote these words to his fiancée.

> When I also think about the situation of the world, the complete darkness over our personal fate and my present imprisonment, then I believe that our union can only be a sign of God's grace and kindness, which calls us to faith. We would be blind if we did not see it. Jeremiah says at the moment of his people's great need "still one shall buy houses and acres in this land" as a sign of trust in the future. This is where faith belongs. May God give it to us daily. And I do not mean the faith which flees the world, but the one that endures the world and which loves and remains true to the world in spite of all the suffering which it contains for us. Our marriage shall be a yes to God's earth; it shall strengthen our courage to act and accomplish something on the earth.

Something in me kept reading and rereading that passage; I kept it on my desk as I looked at the various books of Simone Weil, and at pictures of her, and as I remembered her brother's remarks about her – her saintly vocation and her occasional moments of humor, as when she told him once that she'd kept a Jesuit up for hours in a most burdensome conversation. "God has put me here to do this to Jesuits, drive them to distraction!"

The contrast between Simone Weil at the end of her life and Bonhoeffer's affirmation of life at a comparable moment is all too striking. One wishes she had recognized the Old Testament beauty and wisdom expressed in Bonhoeffer's letter. One wishes that she might have forsaken some, just some, of that austerity, that headlong rush to a worldly exit, and stayed with us, nourished us with her splendid moral sensibility, and, finally, trusted God to know when her time had come. But such speculations about what might have been are a distraction from the work she accomplished, from the ideas and examples she left. With affectionate respect, I take on some of these challenges in the following chapters.

In order to have the strength to contemplate affliction, when we are afflicted we need supernatural bread.

Gravity and Grace

A single piece of bread given to a hungry man is enough to save a soul — if it is given in the right way.

The Virgin's milk, the Father's seed — I shall have it if I cry for it.

First and Last Notebooks

Her Hunger

Among the mysteries of Simone Weil's life, her manner of dying has attracted a great deal of attention. In the last year of her life she yearned for a position in the French underground and repeatedly announced that personal jeopardy would be no obstacle to her, but might be desirable. "I would willingly undertake a mission of sabotage," she wrote from New York to her old friend and classmate Maurice Schumann, who was working with Charles de Gaulle at the Free French headquarters. "And as for the transmission of general instructions [in Nazi-occupied France, to members of the Resistance], I would be all the more suitable for that because I only left France on May 14 of this year [1942] and was in contact with the underground movements. In particular I know well, since I have worked with him, the organizer of the paper *Les Cahiers du Temoignage Chrétien* . . . I beg you to get me over to London. Don't leave me to die of grief here."[1]

This was not her only plea to be permitted to risk her life in the French Resistance. Until she entered the hospital in 1943, she kept hoping that she would be sent on a dangerous errand into the French part of the fascist wilderness. Instead she was given the job of reading reports written by various members of the Free French movement — statements about the future of France after the war ended. She complied and evaluated them, adding her own notions about what the nation ought to do to recover morally as well as socially, economically, and politically. But she was mightily frustrated.

She was also getting sicker. Already weak and extremely thin, she went to the doctors. After diagnosing her tuberculosis, they tried, as noted, to cure her by the only mode of treatment then available: bed rest and so-called hypernutremia – lots of calories, food rich in vitamins, minerals, protein. Even today, with antibiotics, she would have presented a formidable difficulty to her doctors, because a major infection requires nourishing meals. In the words of the poet-physician William Carlos Williams, "Tuberculosis patients are burning up – it's the disease – and you have to keep adding to their supply of fuel, or the engine dies."[2]

No doubt her doctors explained to Simone Weil what ailed her and what she required. No doubt, too, she fully understood them. Her powerfully rational mind was never awed or perplexed by science. She understood the laws of physics and chemistry. There was no problem of communication. The doctors wanted her to eat well, but she would not. What seemed to hospital personnel a reasonable request may have struck this patient as an intrusion, or maybe not really to the point.

No one is in a position to know what this terribly sick woman had in mind when she resisted her doctors. They would ultimately call her a suicide, assuming that her meager food intake accelerated her tuberculosis. (Of course, that disease has also taken the lives of many men and women who did everything their doctors requested.) I rather suspect that, had friends and family been present, it still might have been hard for them to obtain a clear and forthright statement of her reasons for refusing so much of the food offered her.

Before she left Marseille for America, and before she contracted tuberculosis, she was haunted by the fact that many of her French countrymen, under the heel of the Nazi conqueror, were living on meager rations. When she told some friends that she had decided to eat no more than other French citizens were able to eat, as a gesture of solidarity, she may well have exaggerated their deprivation, as her lifelong friend and biographer Simone Pétrement speculates.[3] Pétrement also reports that "on arriving in New York she had said to her parents, 'I will not eat more than in Marseille.'"[4] One wonders why a woman then thirty-two years old, able to be so impressively self-sufficient as a thinker and such a proud loner politically, would make such a vow to her parents. There is a stunning discrepancy between Simone Weil's assertive autonomy and her continued dependence on her parents, even into her fourth decade of life.

Her puzzling attitude toward her own well-being is reflected also in a letter Simone Weil wrote to her brother well before she had any idea she would be leaving Marseille for America. In March of 1941 the Weils learned that André and his wife, Eveline, had arrived in America, and Simone wrote to her brother there. "Being in France, the stories for instance about famine don't upset me: even if a real famine occurred, I would undergo it like the others and my imagination would not be unduly affected by it."[5] In the same letter she avers a disinterest in taking refuge in America, where just about everyone in her situation, of course, wanted desperately to go. "Their hospitality [that is the Americans she had been mentioning] is a purely philanthropic matter, and it is repugnant to me to be the object of philanthropy . . . It is more flattering, taking it all in all, to be the object of persecution."

Such a jolting flash of insight erodes conventional thought. Spiritual growth, she meant to say, is strengthened by an act of defiance: to stand up to persecution, rather than to lean on philanthropy. Backbone emerges from a vigorous self-defense – for a colonial people, for instance, or for a child in a family. She was calling attention to the passivity of being on the dole – or, ironically, of being for too long a dependent, at home and at work. Still, in the immediate context of the 1940s, Simone Weil's remark seems absurd. Refugees by the millions craved escape, at any and all costs – a chance to live, a chance to snatch their families from the persecutions of a satanic führer. In the face of such a reality her concern about being on the receiving end of philanthropy makes no sense. For countless people all over the world such dependence is a sad but continuing condition of everyday existence. The nerve, one might say, if not the deadly pride, of a person who dares set herself aside from the rest of the world and says that she would prefer "to be the object of persecution" rather than help from others.

Yet Simone Weil chose her words carefully in her many letters, and indeed they were a central instrument of her intellect, a primary means for her of figuring out what she believed and how she intended to behave. While still with her parents, and on French soil, she had contemplated the desirability of persecution as an alternative to philanthropy, of extreme suffering at the hands of the Nazis as an alternative to the welcoming safety the United States offered all too few potential emigrés during those wartime years. As outraged as this side of Simone Weil would have made so many of her European contemporaries, there had been at work in her a tradition of sacrifice which might help explain her attitude. This is the Simone Weil who, as a child of five in 1914, refused sugar, because she knew the French soldiers fighting the Germans lacked it; the Simone Weil who, as a young woman, restrained her appetite as a gesture of loyalty to France's poor and unemployed: she would eat no more than the unemployment allowance enabled her fellow citizens. Her last-ditch refusal to eat heartily in the tuberculosis sanatorium was perfectly consistent with a lifetime of austerity and compassion. Even at the end she insisted that she get no more than others, that she share the difficult times of her countrymen as concretely as possible.

Even so, there is reason to argue, she took her life; she effectively handed over her body to the tubercle bacillus without so much as a fight. Such being the case, she was whatever someone is, psychiatrically, who commits suicide. Or was she, in modern clinical language, suffering from anorexia nervosa? This diagnosis has been proposed as a way to consider her death, perhaps her entire life. Her early childhood interest in food restriction kept on, though rationalized, in later life. One difficulty with this label, however, and an important one, is that most anorectics don't report a *lifetime* history of food restriction. They tend to be women of middle-class background, like Simone Weil, who as children were apparently "normal" with respect to eating or had a tendency to overeat. In our discussions of this issue, Anna Freud once remarked, "Many anorectic women were once somewhat overweight – and for a considerable time, contentedly so." Their difficulty, she continued, began "when they started on a moderate diet, and the diet ended up taking control of their lives, for reasons they can't explain, nor can anyone else close to them."

These observations do not seem to fit. Simone Weil was not at all like any anorectic patient I have met or treated, or any whom my colleagues who work regularly with anorectic women have described. "Anorexia nervosa is a syndrome characterized by extreme weight loss, body-image disturbances and an intense fear of becoming obese. What begins as a moderate effort to lose weight escalates to a preoccupation with being thin, associated with a profound change in eating habits."[6] Some patients will eat practically nothing, and then use diuretics or laxatives to cause lower readings on the scale, which becomes a veritable moral clock, its calibrations holding for each individual a significance all their own.

I have heard anorectic patients called an assortment of psychiatric and psychoanalytic names, but emphasis on the "narcissistic component" is invariable. When I sought help from Anna Freud on both anorexia in general and on Simone Weil's troubles, I heard, as usual, the caution of a wise, elderly woman and her clinical restraint, her personal as well as professional tact.

> "I suppose some of us would want to say that, a priori, anyone who curtails food drastically, to the point of threatening to lose her life in so doing, is in some serious way crazy, in the vernacular sense of the word. Even if the person seems to be in normal touch with the world otherwise, this excess of self-denial – with the notion, at the same time, of being overweight, or in danger of becoming overweight – is in a sense psychotic thinking. But Simone Weil doesn't seem to have had any delusions of obesity, or at least, hasn't described her *fatness* as the enemy.
>
> "I am afraid that with her we are dealing with a mind so complex, and with an intelligence so refined and symbolic, that the

only way we can know that she didn't really fear obesity, like all other anorectics, would be to listen to her talk in analysis and see what her mind keeps doing with her own ideas and metaphors and similes. . . . But she cannot be a candidate for psychoanalysis! Nor would she have been, I'm sure, had we offered to consult and treat her back then. [Both these remarkable women were in London during 1942 and 1943.] So, I don't think we ought to call her anything clinical, only read her essays and letters and try to figure out what kept pushing its way into her mind – well, not a good way of saying it! I mean, we ought try to see the world as she did and try to understand what she felt and said, and why. She was articulate, and she was determined, and if she was also sick – in her head first, and later, her body – then we'd better be careful about how we refer to that sickness. Even with patients we've known for years – had in analysis for years – we find ourselves changing our minds, pursuing new leads, realizing that what seemed obviously important was not at all that important!"

One of her doctors called Simone Weil "the most difficult patient I have ever seen," and some of us who have tried to understand her thought, never mind her psychology, as it intersected with her body's medical history, have heard within ourselves a similar cry of frustration.[7] There they were, trying to prevail over a serious illness, and there she was, seemingly oblivious to their struggle because of her own. But what was she struggling to be, to do, to make known to herself, to others? Again, the mystery, the unanswerable – and yet, there are clues in her writing which indicate that for her eating was a highly charged matter, connected in her mind to religious imagery of commanding importance.

"Religion is a form of nourishment," she asserts in "Forms of the Implicit Love of God," an essay written in April of 1942. She adds, "It is difficult to appreciate the flavor and food value of something one has never eaten." She had, herself, "eaten" rather earnestly of religion, though with questionable satiety. In the same essay she offers this general description of religious longing.

In the period of preparation the soul loves in emptiness. It does not know whether anything real answers its love. It may believe that it knows, but to believe is not to know. Such a belief does not help. The soul knows for certain only that it is hungry. The important thing is that it announces its hunger by crying. A child does not stop crying if we suggest to it that perhaps there is no bread. It goes on crying just the same. The danger is not lest the soul should doubt whether there is any bread, but lest, by a lie, it should persuade itself that it is not hungry. It can only persuade itself of this by lying, for the reality of its hunger is not a belief, it is a certainty.

Though her wording may strike a modern reader of no special religious sensibility as dramatic, unnerving, even troublesome in its psychological "content," similar passionate and desperate exhortations of self, or lamentations, were made by Augustine and John of the Cross, whom she mentions in the essay from which the above quotes are taken. She was deeply versed intellectually as well as emotionally in their religious and literary tradition. Hunger and nourishment were her chosen metaphors, and she works with them relentlessly, starkly. It is one thing to think of religion as "nourishment" – a comparison many secular agnostics of psychological sophistication would find congenial – but the persistence with which she pursues the analogy might alarm such readers.

How can we move from belief based on faith to a conviction whose premises we can truly respect? Simone Weil makes the dilemma vivid in this characteristic imagery. She isn't at all interested in the intellectual arguments about whether God "really" exists and how we "really" can distinguish between what we believe and what we, for sure, know to be. "The soul knows for certain only that it is hungry," she has declared – a blunt and brief and powerful assertion, followed by a new image, that of the child crying out of hunger, crying for bread. This crying, she insists, is a reality, and we are in great jeopardy if we refuse to acknowledge such a personal (existential) condition. She will not say we are misleading ourselves or that we are being foolish or stupid or stubbornly uncomprehending. We lie.

There is in her analysis an austerity and severity that carries a twentieth-century mind back almost to the doors of those desert fathers who were so relentlessly self-critical. Today's psychoanalyst would connect the words *hunger* and *lie* and take note of the accusatory link and the comparison to a baby crying. Many of my students, who happen not to have read *Waiting for God*, but rather *The Need for Roots* and other of Simone Weil's more political writings, are moved to think of her as "a voice crying in the wilderness." Though that phrase most certainly does justice to her anarchistic politics, there was about her not only a determined individualism but a deliberate estrangement, as if she weren't *enough* alone. If she were truly, *desirably* hungry and committed to enduring that hunger as an aspect of her trek toward God, she would no longer be a wailing child who is hungry, but a gratefully hungry pilgrim.

The famished seeker is in turn being sought by a God Simone Weil has dared portray in some detail. This time the hunger is God's. "God is longing to come down to those in affliction," she advised herself, and at another point she reminded herself that "in the great symbols of mythology and folklore, in the parables of the Gospels, it is God Who seeks man." Through an extended metaphor in the same essay she tells us more about this God, His way of meeting us.

> The beauty of the world is the mouth of a labyrinth. The unwary individual who on entering takes a few steps is soon unable to find the opening. Worn out, with nothing to eat or drink, in the dark, separated from his dear ones, and from everything he loves, and is accustomed to, he walks on without knowing anything or hoping anything, incapable even of discovering whether he is really going forward or merely turning round on the same spot. But this affliction is as nothing compared with the danger threatening him. For if he does not lose courage, if he goes on walking, it is absolutely certain that

he will arrive at the center of the labyrinth. And there God is waiting to eat him. Later he will go out again, but he will be changed, he will have become different, after being eaten and digested by God. Afterward he will stay near the entrance so that he can gently push all those who come near into the opening.[8]

A little further on we learn that "the beauty of the world is Christ's tender smile for us coming through matter." How could someone who was so knowledgeable about mathematics, physics, astronomy, and, indeed, the general principles of science, have ended up writing in such a manner? A paradoxical or mystical turn of a brilliant mind? Another interpretation, of course, is psychiatric — projecting a mix of the devouring and the tender into cosmic significance.

In the *Dark Night of the Soul*, Saint John of the Cross, who imposed suffering on himself in penance and also suffered from the malicious will of others, warns of "spiritual gluttony."

For some of these persons, attracted by the pleasure which they find therein, kill themselves with penances, and others weaken themselves with fasts, by performing more than their frailty can bear, without the order or advice of any, but rather endeavoring to avoid those whom they should obey in these matters; some, indeed, dare to do these things even though the contrary has been commanded them.

Simone Weil read deeply of John of the Cross and surely noted the irony of that term "spiritual gluttony." Yet she remained determined to struggle with her flesh as mightily as John did. In a revealing passage written as part of a brief essay, "Detachment," and ultimately published posthumously as part of *Gravity and Grace*, she ponders "two ways of renouncing material possessions." One would be "to give them up with a view to some spiritual advantage" — a wrongheaded, sly maneuver, she believed, as did her beloved John of the Cross. Alternatively, one might "conceive of them [material possessions] and feel them as conducive to spiritual well-being (for example: hunger, fatigue, and humiliation cloud the mind and hinder meditation) and yet to renounce them." She adds, "Only the second kind of renunciation means nakedness of spirit"; and a bit further, "We must give up everything which is not grace and not even desire grace."

This dialectical turn of mind is relentless in its tenacity. In her darkly earnest attempt at "decreation," she strives to "pass into the uncreated"; she announces that "we only possess what we renounce"; she pleads, "May God grant that I become nothing"; she explains that "we must become nothing, we must go down to the vegetative level; it is then that God becomes bread." Presumably, at that point she could, at last, eat – though she would no longer be Simone Weil. She is ready and willing to be "vegetative" – or beyond. "It would be better to be the mud which obeys God, rather than someone who could be like God."⁹

As I read such passages to Anna Freud, she showed less alarm than I had expected. She first remarked at her "ignorance." "I don't know enough about this person, even though these words of hers certainly tell me something – give me pause! My ignorance of her tells me to keep my speculations to a minimum. As I listened to you reading those truly grim passages, I wondered whether the one who wrote them did so grimly, or with the confidence of an essayist. You say she was alone and sick here in London, and we had the blitz, then, I remember. On the other hand, she is using a complex mind in a rather artful fashion. . . . I kept wondering to myself: To whom was this young lady speaking? She doesn't address God Himself. She speaks *of* Him, rather than *to* Him, mostly. She isn't addressing herself, only – it is not really a *cri de coeur*, a person in great anguish. She is giving us 'pensées,' a series of brief, didactic essays. But they are part of her journals, and they are jottings, in a sense – her mind talking to itself. On the other hand, so many of my patients who have kept diaries or journals have ended up saying that they have finally realized who it is – the one they have sought to address!"

I think it fair to say that we both had an inclination to push ahead in a conventional psychoanalytic manner and to apply psychological imagery to all this metaphysical and mystical imagery. Anna Freud resisted this inclination. Phrases such as "parental imago," or "superego" don't quite work, and the thought of a child imploring her parents, or standing up to them (I can do without your offerings, your food and clothing, your anything and everything!) is not at all to be equated with the reality of a writer who had at her command a lineage that includes not only the monks John of the Cross describes critically, and John himself, but Juliana of Norwich and Teresa of Avila, and Pascal, whose scientific brilliance did not stop him from being aphoristic in a religious vein.

It is worth remembering that this was a young *woman*, one who urgently wanted to put her considerable moral energy at the service of her country and could find no way of so doing that satisfied her demanding conscience. Had she been a man she might well have been able to fight the Nazis, even coax her superiors into parachuting her onto French soil. Bonhoeffer could take his stand, as could other men who fought Hitler in this or that underground. Like other women, Simone Weil was expected to stand back and wait – surely a maddening constraint for a person of such intensity, such mighty resolution. Perhaps this last frustration reminded the woman Simone of the child Simone, who was required to be a good and proper girl rather than the strong and independent person her mind and spirit made her. It was no great leap, for her, from that sense of futility, that feeling of uselessness, that rage at being judged odd for wishing to be an active fighter, never mind for dreaming of a future France far better than its past incarnation to another sense: of embittered hopelessness. Maybe she was, yes, fed up, eager to leave this life for another. Her psychology nourished her religious aspirations – at the terrible expense of her earthly life.

During that same conversation, after we had put aside Simone Weil's writing and diverted ourselves with coffee and cake, Anna Freud shook her head and wondered out loud, with obvious mercy in her voice, "whether there was any pleasure in all that tense thinking of hers." Then she smiled, commented on how delicious the cake was, and on the joy a strong cup of coffee can bring — the taste, the warmth, and soon enough, the invigorating lift. Was there any satisfaction even remotely similar available to this virginal and abstemious woman who slept little and dreamed night and day, in her last years, of martyrdom on her French soil? I was at a loss for words, but found myself groping for the Pétrement biography of Simone Weil. There I came upon this passage:

> Using masked, circuitous language, she mentioned her "request for a post," that is, her desire to go to England; and she also spoke about the ideas that had come to her "concerning certain passages in Tacitus," that is, her project for a group of front-line nurses. (She had in fact discovered in Tacitus that the ancient Germans had the custom of placing a young girl surrounded by an elite of young warriors in the front lines during a battle.)

With that we both laughed — with relief. After tiptoeing around the questions all this imagery of starvation and sacrifice raised (what kind of childhood did this woman have, as a prelude to her journey into self-effacement, into decreation?), we could enjoy this self-enhancing and self-displaying fantasy. There was a delicious minor irony in the ancient German woman's warrior life prompting a dream or two in a modern French woman's mind. And where did she find this dream but in Tacitus — she who made such derisive attacks on Rome, never finding anything worthwhile to say about it or its writers or heroes.

Anna Freud leaned back in her chair and said, "She is a combative writer." We agreed that it was hard to earn her respect — hard for Simone Weil herself or for anyone else, unless you were an ancient Greek. The further back she goes into history, the more tolerant she becomes. Her genius was to pick up flaws and weak spots — and to propose brilliant utopias.

In her New York notebook of 1942, Simone Weil stated that "a single piece of bread given to a hungry man is enough to save a soul – if it is given in the right way." Yet she seemed thoroughly unable and unwilling to allow herself to take that "single piece of bread." One wonders about her notion of spiritual charity, given the fierce assault she launches on every aspect of ordinary being in the *Gravity and Grace* essays. True, the progression from detachment and self-effacement to decreation, the renunciation she mentions, can be her version of the necessary and important battle against pride, that sin of sins for both Old and New Testament writers. Yet this assault on being seemed part of a different battle.

Anna Freud and I settled on the phenomenological use of the phrase "eating disorder," saying – without reductive smugness, I hope – that for all save a small number of individuals on this planet, as even Simone Weil reminded herself, "if one is hungry one eats." The refusal to do so is, therefore, statistically an aberration: the marked departure from what holds for almost everyone else.

Long before Simone Weil suffered the fever of tuberculosis, it was as if an intense fire burned in her and made her struggle restlessly. Frustrated libido comes to mind, naturally – the old physics of the late nineteenth century transferred by Freud to the mind's life: instinctual energy damned, hence turned inward, with a consequent fire of language: God as a word, an idea, loved in letters and essays, in prayer and thought. "Only God is the good," she tells herself (warns herself?) in her New York notebooks, "therefore only He is a worthy object of care, solicitude, anxiety, longing, and effort of thought." The "therefore" is her notion of what must follow, of course, and arguably, nowhere is she more aberrant spiritually from her beloved Jesus than at this point. He, who ministered eagerly, lovingly to the poor and the exiled and the imprisoned, never asking of them proof of "the good." Each of them was "a worthy object" of His "care, solicitude, anxiety, longing, and effort of thought."

She seemed bored with the moral infractions we all commit; her conscience reached for an absolutism utterly unqualified. Any id faced with such a superego will find all daily life forbidden. But an agile, knowing, inventive ego can spring instinct into a universe beyond all flesh, a universe impossible to approximate with words, hence the opacity, if not the murky deterioration of language and thought in some of those notebook pages. The fits and starts, the aborted memos to the self, the dense and extremely condensed warnings make Pascal's *Pensées* seem positively expansive, accessible: "The unconditioned is contact with God. Everything that is conditioned is of this world. (Ex. Jacob: If . . . if . . . if . . . *then* shall the Lord be my God.) The unconditional is the absolute."

What of contact with the flesh – the stomach, for instance? "God alone is worthy of interest and absolutely nothing else," the writer has declared in her notebook only a page or so earlier, and she has "absolutely" no intention of yielding to compromise. If God had the ideas about Himself that she had with respect to Him, then an ultimate, a divine narcissism would rule the universe. But Simone Weil, like Karl Barth, regarded God as not without desire – a sort of hunger for us creaturely folk, a search on His part that nicely balances our own for Him.[10]

Another of Anna Freud's warnings comes to mind: "A figure such as Simone Weil is likely to teach as much through your 'gut reaction' to her, if examined, as by your head's analysis of her writing." I remember joking, feebly, that our guts probably will fill with acid, with bile as we think of another's gut so chronically empty, and read that such a state of affairs was considered to be a real ethical achievement. "'Thou shalt not eat . . . ' 'Thou shalt not open,' 'Thou shalt not think.' Fortunate is he who is capable of obeying such orders." Clearly the author of those words was more successful in curbing her appetite than her thinking. In this respect the very statement is a direct challenge to a negative injunction, as if one held a hot fudge sundae in one's hand while extolling the one who does "not eat."

No doubt even a sustained textual analysis of every single reference Simone Weil ever made to food, to hunger, and to eating in her letters, her journals, and her essays, would continue to puzzle us. So much of her thinking resists conventional categories, modes of analysis. In the New York notebooks, at one point, she declares,

"If one is hungry one eats, not for the love of God but because one is hungry." But then, right away, she adds a concrete, existential situation that begins to hedge. "If an unknown man lying in the road is hungry one must give him food, even if one has not enough for oneself, not for the love of God, because he is hungry." She adds that such a gesture "is what it is to love one's neighbor as oneself." But she won't let the matter drop there; she is not content to acknowledge the simple fact of hunger as an aspect of our mortality, qualified by our ethical obligation to think of others who also know hunger. She is not satisfied with this brief but important lesson in practical ethics. "To give 'for God,' to love one's neighbor 'for God' or 'in God,' is not to love him as oneself. One loves oneself by an effect of animal feeling. . . . This animal feeling is a contradiction. Miraculous. Supernatural." She is aware that egoism, by definition, has its bounds; it cannot become transcendent. "One judges the self-love which nature implants deep in the soul to be legitimate insofar as one is the creature of God."[11]

She is engaged here in an impressive struggle for an approving nod from on high, for the vindication of "animal feeling." But the outcome, a judgment of legitimacy, was a costly one. Hunger keeps asserting itself, round the clock, day after day; if one can't let it be, as she starts out doing ("If one is hungry one eats"), but rather, has to mobilize a constant philosophical and theological effort, then even exhausting factory work of which she wrote with such hurt and sadness may seem, in comparison, a pleasant diversion. When thinking overshadows eating, the latter becomes a self-conscious act rather than an animal feeling. Her ego, to call on the constructs of psychoanalysis yet again, was not about to surrender itself to the demands of the id, or of the superego, either. Well-muscled and energetic, her ego moved with agility, one minute saying yes, of course, to instinct, the next bringing up with a vengeance the question of what is right, what is justifiable, legitimate. If someone like this were in therapy one might work for a release, a negotiated truce that allowed for unself-consciousness:

37

Since one *is* a "creature of God" then – well, one can get on with it, with living, at breakfast, lunch, and dinner.

If hunger prompts continual thought, continual moral analysis – a striving to link one's narcissism with God's creative energy – the energy expended may be out of all proportion, leaving little for eating and sleeping, and never mind sleeping with anyone. In her last months of life, Simone Weil was feverishly at work writing; she saw few people and slept and ate little. As she wrote "The Needs of the Soul," posthumously to be a major part of *The Need for Roots*, her imperialist ego had triumphed over the needs of her body.

Maybe a literary rather than a psychiatric analogy is more helpful.[12] Knut Hamsun's first novel, *Hunger*, was published in 1890.[13] He was thirty-one, about the age of Simone Weil when France fell. The novel is an account of a young writer's struggle to be loyal to his private, compelling wishes and dreams. The price was a harsh, unremitting poverty. Norway, at that time, was no welfare state. The hero can call upon no government agency for "benefits." He can only save himself from virtual starvation by taking a job, any job. But he won't; he is a writer, and if he were to stop being one, he would join the living dead. Instead, he lives, goes hungry, pursues his particular destiny, and so doing, becomes melancholy one moment, full of ecstatic plans the next, rational today, confused and clouded tomorrow.

Hunger acts on his mind as well as his body. Indeed, the novel is not so much about hunger as a physical or medical matter as about the interior life that accompanies such a condition – hunger in the tradition of Dostoyevsky's *Notes from Underground*. All the brooding, introspective agony of the late nineteenth-century intelligentsia, all its struggles with the social and political (bourgeois) conformity of that age, are woven into *Hunger*. Even as Hamsun himself has been called a writer "whose foremost passion" turned out to be a "violent, defiant deviation from everything average and ordinary," Simone Weil was determined to question everything all her life. Her unpredictability became an intellectual tic. One can feel her squirming, challenging any regular or accepted

position, any ordinary manner of thinking, any conventional political or religious affiliation. Hamsun's central character in *Hunger*,
interestingly enough, is called a suicide-hero – a young person of
great talent and stubborn creativity who won't bend to the dictates
of his stomach or to middle-class values. In the novel, as in Simone
Weil's life, abstract social standards are put to an intimate
psychophysiological test.

As I read *Hunger*, I understood the difference between the life of
Simone Weil and of Hamsun's hero, on the one hand, and the lives
of obsessed or anorectic patients doctors see so often these days.[14]
No wonder Anna Freud wasn't going to sweep Weil under some
diagnostic label; no wonder she kept emphasizing to me that she saw
no real evidence that Simone Weil was "obsessed" in the way
anorectic patients are, and no real evidence that "her narcissism was
handled by her" the way anorectic women deal with theirs!

"I will never know whether I am right in what I suspect," she
remarked, and continued.

"But this young woman was directing her thoughts *outward*;
there was little in the world that she did not care to notice and
comment upon! You have shown me the extraordinary range of
her personal and intellectual involvements – in such a short life!
This is a narcissism that is not pathologically 'fixed' on her own
appearance and weight and her appetite and her potential obesity. . . . It sounds as if she was careless with herself. I doubt she
had a scale in her room – and maybe not a mirror. My hunch is
that if she had had a mirror, she would have given the mirror
the same trouble she gave a loaf of bread! At the same time, her
heart was ready to travel all over the world, reach out to
everyone, it seems, and carry with it, if she could, her trail,
exhausted body. We all have our narcissism, as you say [I had
made that obvious point in order to ask for more help on the
specific nature of Simone Weil's narcissism], but the different
ways various individuals end up using and reacting to that narcissism is one, among several ways, we can make significant
clinical distinctions about those people."

Anna Freud's remarks about clinical distinctions reminded me of my two years in the air force as a psychiatrist – how the labels of my profession were used to encourage or discourage "behavior" at the behest of the military. We were in no war then, but later some of my colleagues were drafted into the armed services during the Vietnam War. They had the task, in Asia, of helping men go back to duty, to face much better than even chances of dying. Some of those who were "successfully treated" ended up fighting with as much zeal and passion and high idealism as Simone Weil managed to muster in the brief years allotted her, and many came to a lonely, grim death, a match for that endured by her. These men weren't considered "disturbed" for having knowingly risked their lives. No one is writing an article about their passion for martyrdom, their self-punitive tendencies, their strange "compulsion" for repeated self-exposure to death.

I remember hearing Reinhold Niebuhr speak about Dietrich Bonhoeffer, at the Union Theological Seminary in the early 1950s. When Bonhoeffer, as mentioned above, decided to return to Germany and take on the Nazis directly, friends cautioned him, pointing out all he might do in America without risking his life. Niebuhr reminded us how this Aryan aristocrat, who could easily have had the best of just about any world – he could have become a prominent part of Nazi Germany or a prominent anti-Nazi refugee in the United States – had to face the psychological skepticism of those around him. Ought he not go and talk with someone? Might he possibly have a problem, a need to submit to the obvious danger that an anti-Nazi would face in 1939 or 1940? In retrospect, we ask, instead, why so few others were "sick" enough to contend with Hitler and his henchmen in the dedicated and public way Bonhoeffer chose.

Who is to judge? Did Bonhoeffer require psychiatric counsel? Need he have died at the hands of the Nazis, who waited eagerly for the smallest gesture of reconciliation on his part? All he need have done is denounce them from the safety of America, or once in Germany, be a touch more discreet in his disapproval. Just as Simone Weil had dreamed, he "parachuted" into fascist territory, fearlessly took on the Nazis, and died, praying to Jesus. The agonized, passionate spirituality of the letters he wrote to friends and family just before his death was enough to make any stable burgher-psychiatrist raise his eyebrows. Bonhoeffer's "hunger" was for a Germany free of Hitler, and he died loyal to that intense desire.

As for Simone Weil, her hunger was for God, not a slim waistline. She was not the first mystic to be a picky eater. She wanted the quickest possible life consistent with her own tenaciously held ideas. (Once in the Almighty's arms, though, how long would it take her to have an intense argument with Him?) She wanted to live, so she could die in the most honorable manner. She saw herself perhaps shot by the Nazis as her parachute approached the earth — the gravity she constantly mentioned at last banished, her soul rising through grace, leaving the white handkerchief of war far behind. One feels sure that this brave and yet scatterbrained person, as shrewdly sane as could be and as wacky as could be, had a central dream: her moment of release, her giddy ascent, His welcome. Her intense moral imagination simply couldn't stop doing its work, couldn't stop distracting her from the routines the rest of us take for granted, including our meals. She refused the food offered her while awaiting the big feast she often mentioned, the one given the symbolic form of Holy Communion. She yearned to have her appetite appeased, not for a day or for a week, Sunday to Sunday, but forever.

The Hebrews took as their idol, not something made of metal or wood, but a race, a nation, something just as earthly. Their religion is essentially inseparable from . . . idolatry, because of the notion of the "chosen people."

Israel and Rome set their mark on Christianity; Israel by causing the Old Testament to be accepted by it as a sacred book, Rome by turning it into the official religion of the Roman Empire.

Letter to a Priest

3

Her Jewishness

No aspect of the life of Simone Weil is more problematic – and sad – than her attitudes toward her Jewish background. "What is a Jew?" she asked in a letter to the minister of education of the Vichy government in November 1940, six months after France had fallen to the Nazis.[1] The letter was prompted by her unsuccessful attempt to obtain a teaching job. The government of Marshal Pétain had already begun following Hitler's lead; a number of anti-Semitic statutes had been enacted,[2] and she did not receive an appointment. Far be it from her to have let such a situation stand! She reflected, fumed, and then wrote to the minister. The letter begins with a description of her past history of teaching and her most recent request "for a teaching post, preferably in Algeria." That request had not been answered. She wryly suggests to her correspondent that "the new Statute on Jews," of which she had read in the newspapers, "is perhaps connected to your failure to reply." If so, she wanted to know "to whom this Statute applies." She is candid to say that her reason for wanting such information is personal, "so that I may be enlightened as to my own standing.

"I do not know the definition of the word 'Jew,'" she announces and adds, "The subject was not included in my education." Up to this point one might think that she was merely speaking tongue in cheek, restraining her moral disgust, her sense of horror that France had joined the murderous anti-Semitic forces moving

43

through Europe. But no, she moves in another direction, a direction one cannot ignore if one wants to understand her blind spots as well as her virtues.

Having said that her education had failed her with respect to the Jewish question, she turns herself into the vigorous, contentious logician she could often be – in this case an almost perversely meticulous one, arguing as a lawyer rather than a moralist. "The Statute, it is true, defines a Jew as 'a person who has three or more Jewish grandparents,'" she reminds the minister. "But this simply carries the difficulty two generations farther back." She knew perfectly well, of course, that "the difficulty" had nothing to do with genealogy but, as she indicated, was a matter of arbitrary definition. (In Germany, only *one* Jewish grandparent was enough to clinch the matter for men, women, and children.)

"Does this word [Jewish] designate a religion?" she asks, again ingenuously. Was this the feigned innocence of a brilliant intellectual who actually thought about, if she did not worry over, just about everything? But no, she now eagerly pleads her cause. "I have never been in a synagogue, and have never witnessed a Jewish religious ceremony. As for my grandparents – I remember that my paternal grandmother used to go to the synagogue, and I think I have heard that my paternal grandfather did so likewise. On the other hand, I know definitely that both my maternal grandparents were free-thinkers. Thus, if it is a matter of religion, it would appear that I have only two Jewish grandparents, and so am not a Jew according to the Statute."

This is an extraordinary statement from someone who was constantly attacking arid legalisms of all kinds – any effort to live by the letter rather than the spirit. Perhaps, one keeps hoping, she was sarcastically playing a numbers game: not three, but two, and so count me out, not in. But even had she won her case, with whom would she have been keeping company? The Vichy racists, rather than the Jews, or the Christians of France who not only opposed such statutes, but declared themselves ready to share the pain with those to whom they were meant to apply, a reaction one might also have expected of Simone Weil. As for the reference to her maternal grandparents, she knew that proudly self-described Jews – Freud, for instance – had also been strong free thinkers for quite some time in Germany and France and England – the assimilated Diaspora of Western Europe. Why, then, pose free thinking as a negation of one's Jewishness?

She then moves directly to the awful heart of the matter. "But perhaps the word designates a race?" she asks, knowing that Hitler's fondest hope had been, for years, that the world at large regard Jews in exactly that way, as a race, an abominable Jewish race.

> In that case I have no reason to believe that I have any link, maternal or paternal, to the people who inhabited Palestine two thousand years ago. When one reads in Josephus how thoroughly Titus exterminated this race, it seems unlikely that they left many descendants. My father's family, as far back as our memory went, lived in Alsace; no family tradition, so far as I know, said anything about coming there from any other place. My mother's family comes from Slavic lands, and, so far as I know, was composed only of Slavs. But perhaps the Statute must be applied to my grandparents themselves, perhaps we must now investigate whether each of them had less than three Jewish grandparents? I think it may be quite difficult to get reliable information on this point.

No doubt there is irony at work here, but not a cool and relaxed kind; rather, the writer is brittle and all too self-protective as she tries to shake off the reality of her ancestral tradition. She knew quite well that her family on her mother's side was made up of Russian Jews, on her father's of Franco-German Jews. She knew that these so-called Ashkenazic Jews go back centuries. Few historians would accept her preposterous, though revealing, assertion that this Jewish race was at a certain point "exterminated." While she may have been arguing to confront the Vichy authorities with their wrongheadedness, she was trying too hard at the task, perhaps in an effort to convince herself.

45

In her conclusion, she goes far beyond the sardonic, again becoming personal and autobiographical.

> Finally, the concept of heredity may be applied to a race, but it is difficult to apply it to a religion. I myself, who profess no religion and never have, have certainly inherited nothing from the Jewish religion. Since I practically learned to read from Racine, Pascal, and other French writers of the 17th century, since my spirit was thus impregnated at an age when I had not even heard talk of "Jews," I would say that if there is a religious tradition which I regard as my patrimony, it is the Catholic tradition. In short: mine is the Christian, French, Greek tradition. The Hebraic tradition is alien to me, and no Statute can make it otherwise.

Further light on her attitudes toward Judaism is shed by a letter she wrote her brother, André, in September 1942. Her only niece, Sylvie, had just been born, and she was quick to recommend baptism for the infant.

> I would not hesitate for a second, if I had a child, to have it baptized by a priest. There would be only one reason to hesitate: if the child might regret it later on. Sylvie would not have the shadow of a reason to regret having been baptized by a priest unless she later turned toward a fanatical Judaism, which isn't very probable. If she turns to atheism, Buddhism, Catharism, Hinduism, or Taoism, what would it matter to her that she had been baptized? If she turns to Christianity, Catholic or Protestant, which is indeed her right, she will be very happy about it. If her fiancé is a Jew, an atheist, Buddhist, etc., her baptism will not be an inconvenience; she will not be responsible for it. If a more or less anti-Semitic piece of legislation grants advantages to baptized half-Jews, it will be agreeable for her, probably to enjoy these advantages without having done anything cowardly. In summation, I believe that if she is not baptized, in twenty years she will wish she had been.[3]

Simone Weil, who never let herself be baptized, who wrote at length about her conflicting sentiments with respect to that act, has no such qualms for her niece, though she does allow that the child might one day "regret" the decision. For one who was constantly worrying about the rights of people, their need to be protected from the intrusions of others, might this not have been a moment for consideration, for reflection, rather than swift decisiveness?

As for the phrase "fanatical Judaism," it is stark evidence of her blindness on this subject. Couldn't she imagine that a person of Jewish ancestry might have misgivings about a baptism in childhood? Mightn't she have conceived that a grown-up Sylvie could someday meet and fall in love with a Jewish man, and that those two young people might have a bit of concern about her baptism? Couldn't she imagine that Sylvie herself might take an interest in the spiritual side of Jewish life and wish to embrace that life without being a fanatic?

But most telling of all, alas, is the sentence in which Sylvie is described as half-Jewish (after all that hemming and hawing to the Vichy minister!). Most astonishingly, her baptism is recommended on the grounds that if she lived in a country where anti-Semitic laws prevailed, she would enjoy, as a baptized Catholic, "advantages" without being considered "cowardly." Simone Weil, this powerful moralist, usually so courageous, if not heroic, is crassly talking about the advantages someone might someday enjoy under an anti-Semitic government. How does one comprehend such a striking departure from the rest of her thought?

Toward the end of her life, when Simone Weil was working for the Free French under General de Gaulle, she received "texts of various kinds" from members of the Resistance. These were evaluated by various members of de Gaulle's staff and by her. A number of these reports, as Simone Pétrement mentioned in her biography, have not yet been, and some may never be, published.[1] One which she evaluated dealt with "the bases for a statute regarding French non-Christian minorities of foreign origin"; it may well be judged unworthy of publication. Here is how Pétrement, a loyal and strong friend of Simone Weil's, describes that assignment.

The authors of this project, while refuting various accusations leveled against them [the Jews], considered it an irrefutable fact that the Jews constituted a distinct minority and maintained that due to this the majority could legitimately take measures to avoid possible inconveniences, such as, for example, the presence of too many Jews in the administration, or their presence in certain high positions.[5]

Pétrement provides us with Simone Weil's response.

The central idea is correct: that it is a matter not of knowing whether the Jewish minority has this or that characteristic, but whether it exists. Correct also is the idea that this minority has as a common bond the absence of the Christian heritage. However, it is dangerous to consider the accepted premises as stable and to make them correspond to a stable *modus vivendi*. The existence of such a minority does not represent a good thing; thus the objective must be to bring about its disappearance, and any *modus vivendi* must be a transition toward this objective. In this regard, official recognition of this minority's existence would be very bad because that would crystallize it.[6]

Pétrement, in her account of this awful moment in her subject's life and thought, concludes with no comment of her own, only a narrative link from the above quotation to another one.

The measures she considered desirable to facilitate this minority's disappearance, that is, to make it gradually melt into the aggregate of the nation, are mainly: "the encouragement of mixed marriages and a Christian upbringing for future Jewish generations. If a genuinely Christian inspiration – without the encroachment of dogma on intelligence – really impregnated the training, education, and upbringing of the youth in France, and even more the entire life of the country, neither the so-called Jewish religion nor the atheism typical of Jews emancipated from their religion would be strong enough to prevent contagion. . . . It is only in relation to inspiration of an authentic spirituality, which has already begun to pervade the life of the country, that protective measures against those incapable of participating would be appropriate."[7]

New paragraph: "The next project concerned . . ." In her sensitive, affectionate study, Pétrement offers no discussion of the implications of this line of thought. As Simone Weil's words were written, one has to remember, the Gestapo was doing its work a few hundred miles to the east — train after train headed for gas chambers and firing squads. I don't think we do Simone Weil justice by glossing over this dark hour in her life, by failing to give it thorough scrutiny. Had she succumbed to the self-hatred of the victim?

I have spent a lifetime hearing certain children say precisely what is said about them by their critics and by their parents' critics. I have heard blacks mouth racist innuendos worthy of the Ku Klux Klan. An Eskimo child once told me he thought "everything will be better when my people disappear." "Identification with the aggressor" is an old story, and not only children fall prey to it. The wondrously literate and discerning Walter Lippmann went along readily with the patronizing anti-Semitism of the president of Harvard University,[8] A. Lawrence Lowell, no less, a decade or two before Simone Weil wrote as she did. Both were astute, and in many ways lucky: born to comfortable, educated parents and recipients of the finest education.

In the case of Simone Weil, one is tempted to expect more: she had no interest in the endless social ingratiation which characterized the life of, say, Walter Lippmann, or so many others, Jewish and non-Jewish, who live in our class-conscious world. She could be so defiantly herself, so truculently willing to mock convention, the determined outsider. Why did such independence fail her in this instance?

What lay behind her deep antagonism to Jewish tradition? Why was she determined to believe that the ancient Jews were especially brutal and mean-spirited? Why did she expend so much of her intelligence and compassion on the Greeks, on the New Testament, and so little on the people who gave the world the rabbi Jesus Christ? Why was she forever linking the ancient Jews and Rome in one unholy, destructive plot? Why did she abhor the Old Testament? "I have always been kept away from Christianity," she once wrote, "because it ranked these stories [of the Old Testament], so full of pitiless cruelty, as sacred texts." She continues in this fashion.

> I have never been able to understand how it is possible for a reasonable mind to look upon the Jehovah of the Bible and the Father invoked in the Gospel as one and the same being. The influence of the Old Testament and of the Roman Empire, whose tradition was continued by the Papacy, are to my mind the two essential sources of the corruption of Christianity.

At another point she tersely declares that "the twofold Hebraic and Roman tradition has in great measure negated, for two thousand years, the divine inspiration of Christianity."[9]

Intellectually, there is nothing new in the above. The heretic Marcion, in the second century after Christ's death, insisted that there were two gods, one the kindly and lovable Father of Jesus and the other the one known as the Jehovah, the Creator of the Old Testament. According to Marcion, the apostles failed to separate Jesus and His Father from the other God, the one worshiped by the ancient Jews. The point was to separate completely the Christianity of the Roman Catholic Church, as it was then becoming consolidated, from that of its Jewish origins, connections, and heritage. For such thinking Marcion was excommunicated. This so-called Marcionite heresy, a kind of gnosticism, aimed at denying the history of Christianity, its roots in a particular era.

In her passionately fanciful manner, Simone Weil kept trying to connect Jesus to the ancient Greeks, to Plato especially, and to separate Christianity from the Romans and Jews. But the position she took can hardly be understood by resort to theological and historical discussion. She is as blind about the Greeks as she is about the Romans and the Jews — ready to forgive or overlook their brutalities, their mistakes, their greed and corruption, and their militarism. In her mind, the purity of the Greek language, and of the life of Jesus (she recited the Lord's Prayer in Greek), is set against the wretched and corrupt flesh, the avarice and cruelty of just about everyone else. The Jews and the Romans, whose failures she relentlessly studied and belabored, are her scapegoats, embodying all the fleshly impulses and desires of mere mortals.

Under less threatening circumstances, she could be less hostile to certain parts of that "Hebraic tradition." She responded favorably to the Book of Job and the later, prophetic tradition in Jeremiah and the Book of Isaiah. But she was not willing to give what was for her the great gift, her "attention" to Jewish history and the Old Testament. She had made her distinctions and lived by them, allowing them to control her thinking. She sought a Christian world; she was drawn to churches, to priests, to Catholic texts and writers. In this regard, it is interesting to read the introduction to *Gravity and Grace* by her friend Gustave Thibon. Thibon tells of receiving a letter in June of 1941 from Father Perrin: "There is a young Jewish girl here, a graduate in philosophy and a militant supporter of the extreme left. She is excluded from the University by the new laws and is anxious to work for a while in the country as a farm hand."[10] The priest hopes his friend will shelter her and help her find such work.

"Thank God, I do not suffer from any *a priori* anti-Semitism," Thibon writes, and then adds, "but what I know from experience of the qualities and faults of the Jewish temperament does not fit in any too well with my own and is particularly ill-adapted to the demands of everyday life together." This man would become a good friend; she entrusted her manuscripts to him before she left for America, in May of 1942. His denial of "*a priori* anti-Semitism," coupled with reference, in the same sentence, to "faults of the Jewish temperament" gives us a notion of the times she lived in. One wonders how she must have felt when Jewishness became a subject of consideration. Thibon describes their initial experience together as "uncomfortable," yet she soon enough won him over. "Never have I felt the word *supernatural* to be more charged with reality than when in contact with her."

What did she feel about him, apart from gratitude and affection? How did her earthy, feisty, shrewdly logical and penetrating mind — never mind its "supernatural" side — respond when she saw herself trying hard to persuade him and everyone else, herself included, that she was as alien to Jewishness as it was to her? Although she claimed to have had no involvement with Jewishness, she was not ready to let the matter rest there. Rather, she insisted on seizing the initiative, like those around her, ever ready to classify Jews and categorize them, if not insult them and worse. Did she feel ashamed and humiliated, irritated, angry, or more and more fearful?

She was no Nazi. She was ready to die fighting Nazis. Yet, Thibon tells us that "she was fond of saying that Hitler hunted Jews and only persecuted them in order to resuscitate under another name and to his own advantage their tribal god, terrestrial, cruel, exclusive. . . . How many times did she not speak to me of the Jewish roots of anti-Semitism!" I wonder whether, during those "many times" Simone Weil, who was literally on the run, headed she knew not quite where, was trying to find her personal bearings, to find acceptance, no matter the moral cost.

She was a great one for insisting that brains were not nearly enough, or money and position, either, or the conventional education so many of us prize so dearly. She also sought out the strength and dignity of labor, and she sometimes found that strength and dignity in particular laboring people. She was usually too wise to blanket any social class with exemption from sinfulness, from serious moral failures. Would that this sense of proportion, this wise judgment had held as she thought about her own long-suffering people.

As I thought about how she might have been feeling as she criticized Judaism and the Jews, I kept going through my clinical experiences, at different times and in different cultures, and came upon a series of exchanges which I had with Jimmy, a black child in Boston, and which I would later discuss at some length with the black psychologists Kenneth and Mamie Phipps Clark and with Anna Freud. The child was brought to my attention when I was working in Dorchester-Roxbury, a ghetto community of Boston, during the late 1960s. A white schoolteacher told me early in 1968 that she was quite worried about a twelve-year-old boy who, she said, "keeps coming up to me to tell me how bad, bad, bad 'the colored' are." When she asked him what he meant by such a claim, he replied quickly and with evident animus, "He tells me that he knows that more stealing and drug dealing are done by his people than by anyone else, and 'they' are always using knives, and they are 'not equal to whites,' that's what he says."

This teacher was, herself, a civil rights activist, but she knew other teachers in the school who had taught the boy in earlier years, and she tended to think that it was they who "got the boy going." What did she mean? She explained the matter in this fashion.

"I've heard what they say in the teachers' room, and I've even heard them talk the same way in their classes and especially while they are standing in the corridors and talking with the kids. They are tough veterans of the old Boston school system, and frankly, they can't stand the black children. . . . They sometimes do get involved with one or two black kids, and that's even more devastating, because when they are hostile, the black kids at least can fight back or ignore them. But when they are friendly, and then tell these kids that 'their people have a lot of attitude problems' – what I heard a teacher tell Jimmy the other day – it's hard for the child to argue. What Jimmy did was keep nodding, I noticed. The teacher smiled at him, and the kid smiled back – and I wanted to cry!"

As I got to know Jimmy better I began to learn how carefully he watched those teachers, how eagerly he noticed what other white people whom he met in stores, in the library, and at the playground had to say. He was a bright, studious lad who aimed to attend college, to become a teacher himself, or so he thought at the age of twelve and thirteen. He admired some of those teachers whom his teacher considered to be "first-class racists," as she once put it.

"I remember our minister telling me God was whispering in my ear to keep studying, because He'd given me the brains to be good in school, and I'd better do my part, meet Him halfway. When I first went to school I knew I was going to like it. I could figure out right away what the teachers wanted us to do, and I just went ahead and did it! Pretty soon, they were calling me smart, and special, and that was great! . . . If there wasn't school and the library, I'd be nothing. I wouldn't know what to do.

"Everyone my age is getting into trouble. . . . You wonder why God lets all this happen! My people, the colored race, we have a lot of growing up to do. My fourth-grade teacher, she took me to the office once, and she said she wanted to talk with me. She said I'm a leader, and one day she hoped I will lead my people. I wasn't sure what she meant, so she told me. She said the colored people have been persecuted, and she's against that; but she said you have to remember that all the other people, the Irish and the Italians and the Jews, they were persecuted, too, and they were poor, but they didn't just sit around feeling sorry for themselves, and they didn't turn into criminals and become violent and go attacking everyone and stealing. They just de-cided to get out of the swamp, to find themselves some higher land, where they could dry out and they could live better, and that's what they did, and that's what we've got to do, and if we don't, then we're going to get into worse and worse trouble, and it'll be our own fault, and whatever happens, we'll have ourselves to blame, and you can't blame others.

"My momma says she hates all the people on this street. She says they're the dirtiest people in the United States of America. She's always trying to get our neighbors to help her clean the hall in our building, but they won't, so she and I do everything, we have to — and then they all mess things up again. The minis-ter says it's our cross, that we have to carry it, and the Lord, Jesus, He'll be watching us, and when we meet Him, then He'll say that we did the right thing, and He's proud of us, and He'll let us stay up there, and be with Him. In Heaven, you're with Jesus all the time, and He's with you, and there's no hassle like you have here, with the drugs and the gangs and everyone doing the wrong thing, all our people, it seems. We find the syringes and the empty packages, the plastic bags; we see blood; we have the rats, and it's not the landlord's fault. He comes here, and he tries to help us clean up, but he says he's getting out, because he can't keep even with all the trash people dump and the windows they break, just for the hell of it, just to show that if they're not holding a knife to someone's throat or pushing a needle into their veins, they're breaking up someone's property.

"Momma says it's what we're like, a lot of black folks. There are the good people we have, too, but our minister says it's very painful, and he's sure the Lord Jesus can't help noticing the way there are lots of empty seats in church on Sunday, and he's sure as can be that lots of people are sleeping and they've been drinking and shooting up. God has to give us some help here, because we've really fallen away from Him, us colored folks; and like they say in church, 'That's the truth, amen.' There are days, I'll be honest, when if I could say a prayer and ask for a favor from God, I'd ask Him to turn me into a white man, and I'd just move away, and I'd never want to come back here."

Such words, extracted from many hours of conversation, remind me, as I struggle with her life, that Simone Weil was not the first and won't be the last person on this planet to feel critical of her background. This boy was earnestly eager to be respected by others. But he was never truly free of "them," of the view of his people he had learned. How was he to escape – not only "them," but his own sense that he was a hostage of sorts to "them," his fate never separate from theirs? He dreamed of disappearance, but he knew that, short of a miracle, he would never realize this dream. The result: moments and longer of anger, resentment, and bitterness – a sense he had that not only he but the entire world – as his teachers, his minister, and his mother more than implied – suffered because of what people like him did, or really, *are*.

Moreover, it is *God* who suffers, too – a contribution of the child's intensely religious upbringing, with its earthy, strongly felt, vernacular theology: Jesus as an observer of us, a judge of us, as well as our Savior, and Jesus as someone whom one constantly hopes to meet, to get to know intimately, to "join." The word *join* was often on his tongue: "I hope I can be good enough to join Him, and then I won't be with these bad folks here anymore, and it's no more being colored and white in heaven; our minister says, it's being 'part of *His* body.'"

Simone Weil also craved disappearance, union with Jesus. She also allowed herself to consider "disappearance" for her own people, the beleaguered Jews of France, of Europe, even as that boy had permitted a mix of his own experience and the judgments of his mother and his teachers and a librarian and a Boy Scout leader and a park playground employee to push him toward a similar kind of thinking. Simone Weil had managed, a generation earlier, to lump together in her mind the entire Jewish Diaspora in a manner all too consistent with the anti-Semitic thought of her time. She kept on jabbing, jabbing at a people, failing to remember what had happened to them, at whose behest, and indeed, turning them into the masters of their own fate, monsters at work running the world (they and the Romans!).

The psychological parallels are all too evident – the capacity both Simone Weil and Jimmy had to take the oppressors' values seriously, to make them her own, his own. On the other hand, the boy was influenced by older, stronger persons, whereas Simone Weil tried hard to be an unmalleable loner – the bright one who gave the back of her hand to her critics, teachers, and colleagues. The boy was made uncomfortable by actual, observable faults in others, faults he had no reason to want to emulate. Weil's criticism of the Jews was a historical fantasy, which she had concocted for herself. The boy made fair distinctions; he recognized strong, good qualities in his churchgoing elders, in his mother's honorable efforts, in contrast to the global swipes Weil could take at the Jews.

Perhaps we are left to speculate that part of Weil's "problem" with her Jewishness was that she always wanted to endure suffering on her own terms, for radical stands *she* had chosen. The Germans forced her into a category, a position she had not chosen, and she refused to identify with others in the same position.

Once I reminded Jimmy of how many other decent and kind people lived right near him, and as we stopped and talked about this person, then that person, he began to soften his categorical generalizations. This embrace of particularity is the strength of many novelists and playwrights, and under other circumstances of Simone Weil. When that boy became a man, a college student, he deplored "all racism, including black racism." Simone Weil never achieved such a dispassionate distance from herself or from her historical "neighbors," her historical "family." Her thrusts at Jewry demean her and have made many of us who admire her cringe.

When I discussed Simone Weil's Jewishness with Anna Freud, her observations strengthened this point of view.

"You must remember to take into account the time of her life. She grew up when Europe was falling apart and when the question of the Jews was a central one for all Europe, due to the rise of fascism everywhere, not only in Germany. When she was developing as a thinker and a writer few people of her social background, Jewish or non-Jewish, could avoid the subject. Then came Hitler's successes, and with them, I'm afraid, a certain legitimacy to the subject; I mean not only in Germany and the countries near it, but all over the world. I mean by 'the subject' the question of 'the special case of the Jews,' as I heard it put in Vienna.

"You are an American from another generation, and that makes a big difference. With Hitler's defeat the surviving Jews of Western Europe had a changed world to face. I suspect that if Simone Weil had lived she might have found other matters to preoccupy her than this one of her Jewishness, or she would have altered the way she thought of that part of herself. I hope so! It is easy, you are right, to speak of her self-hate in an off-hand manner; to let the phrase be the *end* rather than the *beginning* of our discussion. It was true, she had no use at all for her Jewish ancestry, and yet, she couldn't simply walk away from it.

"I don't for a moment think that she ever convinced herself that she wasn't really Jewish, though I don't think she was 'just' taunting the Vichy authorities, making fun of them with her superior intelligence and knowledge and ability to phrase things. I think she wanted to believe what she wrote, but didn't. I also believe – and who can ever have the answers to what someone like her definitely had going on in her mind? – that she had a strong feeling about herself as a Jewess. You note that those Christian friends of hers in the south of France looked at her as a Jewess, and the pictures you have shown me – they are of a Jewess. Like that black child you've been telling me about – there was something she couldn't get away from, unless she died: the way she looked. Didn't you tell me she was denied her request to be parachuted behind the Nazi lines to do undercover work because she looked so obviously Jewish? I suppose – if we want to get speculative about her thinking – that her comparison of the Jews to the Romans was her way of acknowledging the great exertion of force, one of *her* words, on herself: the Jews conquered her, and she wanted to escape, but couldn't.

"But why did she feel so alien about the Jews, rather than closely connected to them? For one thing, she *did* lack a Jewish upbringing. It doesn't seem she was exaggerating or lying when she said she had practically no Jewish religious experience. For another thing, she was in danger, as all Jews were, and she wanted to be in danger in her own way, on her own terms! She certainly was no coward! She didn't want to be curbed because of what others thought she was; she wanted to be curbed because of that which she made clear to others she had become. To a certain extent there is no sense to be made of all this: it is one person's irrationality, and so we keep finding her saying things out of character, though in character, also, because her

character was such that she almost sought for herself some out-
landish or extravagant positions to uphold."

As we had that helpful conversation, I was reminded, suddenly,
of the one time during her brief stay in the United States that
Simone Weil had entered a synagogue – her eager desire to attend
the services of a Harlem synagogue where Ethiopian Jews worshiped. She also expressed a desire to go South, to work in Alabama
among black sharecroppers. It was not a surprising response to
those who have studied her life – her interest was always in the
poorest of the poor, and her inclination was for the dramatic deed.
She had a wide-ranging mind, a hungry mind, a thirsty mind, a
mind more at home with the strange, the different, and the exotic.
It took blacks – the appeal of the odd, the unusual – to get her to
take herself to a synagogue.

Simone Weil may have known more about Jewish life than she
wanted to realize. That is to say, she may have known full well that
Judaism is a religion *of this earth*, a religion which takes open and
honest stock of the here and now and urges its adherents to engage
themselves in that here and now fully and vigorously, as honorably
as their ability allows them to. Judaism is not a penitential religion
or an immediately messianic one; it dedicates itself to each day's,
each year's personal and ethical responsibilities. The Day of Atone-
ment is solemn, extremely serious, and demanding, but it ends, and
then there is a good feast. Each Friday and Saturday there is serious
reflection, self-scrutiny, and attention given to Israel's long past, to
its laws and customs, to the present: how one lives, behaves, and
carries out individual, familial, and religious responsibilities. But
the point is not prolonged suffering, self-flagellation, a life of abstinence or restriction – themes which have attended Christianity all
along. The Jewish faith and the Jewish culture, for all the suffering
Israel's people have experienced over the centuries, the millennia,
is on the whole a lusty, joyous faith, solidly affirming of the life we
have. Might Simone Weil not have known what such a Judaism
meant for her – a quite different alternative to the moral and personal path she chose, or felt driven to choose?

As we talked, Anna Freud brought up a matter we could only sit quietly and ponder – what this Jewess might have been moved to learn about her people's faith had she survived tuberculosis and Hitler and the craziness of the early 1940s, which fed her apocalyptic imagination. Might she, one day, have learned about the Jewish mystical tradition, the Hasidic Jews – might she have taken to the writing of Martin Buber and Gershom Scholem?[11] Might the sight of the Holocaust survivors have prompted deep within her some aching outcry of protest, not only against Hitler – she always wanted to fight him – but against all the hypocrites and liars who were willing to cozy close to some of his attitudes?

These are rhetorical questions. Still, one thinks of Simone Weil's estrangement from so much of this world during her short life and her ultimate, untimely estrangement from all of it, and one wonders whether an attitude toward Jewishness and an abiding hunger which rarely got appeased in the last years of a life weren't of a piece. With more years of life, Simone Weil might have stopped using the Jews as a foil for her fierce desire to assert independence from the conventions and constraints (the "gravity") of this earthly life. She had an extravagant imagination, capable of leaping over events, dates, traditions, and values. She could be, in such pirouettes with history and factuality, thoroughly perverse and dogmatic. "Jahveh made to Israel the same promises as the devil did to Christ,"[12] she notes at one point. Her literary-intellectual mind, suffused with mystical energy and housed in a body increasingly denied its needed nourishment, was an unpredictable loaded cannon, ready to fire at the Jews anywhere, anytime. "The Scriptures themselves contain the clearest proof that long before the time of Christ, at the dawn of prehistoric times, there was a revelation superior to that of Israel,"[13] and we ask where that proof is. Why offer such a recklessly invidious assertion, so imperious and so damaging ultimately to the one who made it? Why, too, express the great and ostentatious admiration for the ancient Egyptians – on what substantive basis, other than her *dislike* of ancient Israel?

Such diatribes are less than edifying. Her reference to the "moral blindness" of the ancient Jews neglects the obvious links between, say, Isaiah's prophecies and what eventually came to happen in the later Israel of Jesus' time. Her historically knowing and able mind refused for even a moment to examine the relationship of the Jews to Jesus – the splits among the Jews, the complexities of a particularly confused historical moment. Simone Weil pays no attention to those Jews who followed Jesus, the disciples and authors of the Gospels. Risking psychological reductionism, one wonders at times whether a few ancient Jewish fishermen didn't present a challenge to her – sibling rivals of sorts, triggering old competition and self-hate.

It is best to mention, also, an old, sad story: the way socially and intellectually "superior" people learn to express their anti-Semitism or racist attitudes; how distance is put in such quarters between the virulent street hatred of storm troopers or Klan members, on the one hand, and those who sit in elegant drawing rooms or clubs or libraries and make clever remarks about the "temperament" of this group, the "disposition" of that one. "Who gains from this?" the normally not especially political Miss Freud asked. Who gains from the capacity of "cultured" people to have their genteel anti-Semitism or racism? "I suppose," she mused, "it's helpful if people can direct their frustration at Jews and not look at those who may be doing all the time what Jews are criticized for doing."

She was implying that for some of Simone Weil's friends and admirers, and for Weil as well, it must have been more uncomfortable to look at the upper social and cultural and commercial echelons of France and of England, to look at the arrogance and the crafty meanness not of "the Jewish temperament," but of that to be found in French high society or in the Catholic Church. We all "gain," Miss Freud was saying, when we find "others" to help us remain blind to what is right nearby, if not within us.

"For the House of Morgan, the Jews have been, maybe still are, a godsend," I once heard Martin Luther King say. He often asked himself why people misunderstand or hate others, and so doing, do themselves so much damage.

"I have begun to realize how hard it is for a lot of people to
think of living without someone to look down upon, really

61

look down upon. It is not just that they will feel cheated out of someone to hate; it is that they will be compelled to look more closely at themselves, at what they don't like in themselves. My heart goes out to people I hear called rednecks; they have little, if anything, and hate is a possession they can still call upon reliably, and it works for them. I have less charity in my heart for well-to-do and well-educated people — for their snide comments, cleverly rationalized ones, for the way they mobilize their political and even moral justifications to suit their own purposes. No one calls *them* to account. The Klan is their whipping boy. Someday all of us will see that when we start going after a race or a religion, a type, a region, a section of the Lord's humanity — then we're cutting into His heart, and we're bleeding badly ourselves. But then, I guess there's lots of masochism around!" [14]

For Simone Weil her Jewishness became a cross, perhaps an unintended instrument in her repeated efforts to follow Jesus by finding herself wrongly judged. She turned on her Jewishness with a vengeance and got some moments of apparent satisfaction. She felt thereby closer to certain individuals, and as a scholar, she felt closer to certain people whom she admired in history: the Cathars, the Egyptians, the Greeks. Their elevation in her mind required large, persistent expenditures of emotional and intellectual energy, energy that might have been used in a more balanced historical inquiry. The Jews, on the other hand, were a catalyst for a soul absolutely bent on leaving the body — leaving a people and its past in a soaring grasp for another world. They deserved better from her. It is sad that Simone Weil did not bring her intelligent, caring comprehension to her own people, her Lord's people.

The whole of Marxism, in so far as it is true, is contained in the page of Plato on the Great Beast, and its refutation is there, too.

The great mistake of the Marxists and of the whole of the nineteenth century was to think that by walking straight on one mounted upward into the air.

The constant illusion of Revolution consists in believing that the victims of force, being innocent of the outrages that are committed, will use force justly if it is put into their hands. But except for souls which are fairly near to saintliness, the victims are defiled by force, just as their tormentors are. The evil which is in the handle of the sword is transmitted to its point. So the victims thus put in power and intoxicated by the change, do as much harm or more, and soon sink back again to where they were before.

The words of the Breton shipboy to the journalist who asked him how he had been able to act as he did: "There was nothing else for it." The purest heroism — more frequent among the poor than elsewhere.

Gravity and Grace

Her Political Life

All through her few adult years, Simone Weil engaged her mind and heart in politics. Though she was always the intellectual, involved with ideas and analysis, she was deeply interested in political action. She turned twenty one in 1930, the first year of W. H. Auden's "low, dishonest decade,"[1] and in the cafés of Paris soon became a presence with which many of France's political intellectuals knew they had to reckon, arguing with, among others, the exiled Trotsky.[2] She was on "the left" in the sense that she approached both political thought and political action with overriding compassion for the poor. Politics enables any of us to declare our priorities — the rights or values which we set above all else. For her politics was a means to act on behalf of people who had little or nothing, to secure more for them, though she knew and stressed how much stake the giver has in any gift to others.

Unlike her dubious rhetoric when engaged in rewriting religious history, her politics was solid. Her political life reveals her at her best: rational, tough-minded, an extremely shrewd observer of classes, castes, and cultures, of nations and empires, as they have exerted themselves on the stage of history. *The Iliad, or the Poem of Force*, one of her best-known pieces of writing, takes a subtle look at the way people keep trying to coerce other people and thereby become, at once, victor and victim. She regarded the lust for power as a constant protagonist in the human drama, and through *The Iliad* she examined that side of our psychology without the gauzy romanticism she so often summoned for ancient Greece. On the battlefield of Troy, she saw the slavery that the aggrandizing use of force imposes on those who catch its contagious fever. Rome was her bête noire, its imperialism repeatedly cited by her as an example of politics as institutionalized brutishness; but before Caesar there were Hector and Achilles and Agamemnon, and it is to her credit that she did not fail to see that force can consume the virtuous as well as be an instrument of tyrants.

Even in 1928, in her late teens, she allowed herself to be preoccupied with the condition of the poor. A gifted philosophy student, she might easily have disregarded the daily struggles of the French trade union movement as irrelevant to her interests — indeed, as harmful distractions from her "higher" calling. But at the École Normale she became involved in *La Révolution Prolétarienne*, a publication of the syndicalist movement. She read Marx eagerly, welcomed his insistent materialist analysis of history, argued for pacifism, and upheld the struggle of workers for more rights and privileges. When she was twenty-three and a philosophy teacher in a girls' lycée she took part in unemployed workers' demonstrations and consequently was transferred. It was a scandal that someone in her position would desire to do such a thing! But even in her early days as a political activist, while fighting, with words and deeds, both employers and the politicians who were at their beck and call, she looked critically at the left and wrote articles that revealed an early, strong resistance to any one political ideology, including that of Marxism.

She looked back in history at the ways workers became the property of a handful of men, but she also saw in the social and political structures of modern society dangers which Marx and Marxism, she was convinced, had failed to take into enough account — for example, the "oppression exercised in the name of management." She realized that a half century earlier, among the various forms of "management," one was the so-called socialist state, another the liberal-capitalist bureaucracy, intent on ameliorating the lives of its citizens through welfare programs of various kinds. It is instructive, in this regard, to read her references to the "American technocrats" who, early in the Roosevelt New Deal era, drew "an enchanting picture of a society in which, with the abolition of the market, technicians would find themselves all-powerful, and would use their power in such a way as to give to all the maximum leisure and comfort possible." She spotted the "utopianism" in such a political development, the "enlightened despotism" it could quickly end up being.

She saw a similar turn in the Soviet state. Despite her intellectual debt to Marx, she did not justify or rationalize or keep discreetly silent with respect to Lenin's version of statist imperialism, as it had become consolidated in the Soviet Union even before the rise of the brutal and monomaniacal Stalin. Well before the "purges" and show trials of the middle 1930s, she saw Stalin as precisely what a giant bureaucratic totalitarianism would produce, all the notions of a transient "dictatorship of the proletariat" not-withstanding. Though today such a perception strikes us as pure common sense, a candid analysis of the thinking of "leftist" intellectuals of all nations during the late 1920s and early 1930s would find this a rare point of view. When she took to the streets on behalf of the jobless, she also argued on those streets and in editorial offices with others on the same side. They would end up, she was convinced, being as ruthlessly manipulative of the jobless in the name of their political cause as were those who refused to pay decent wages or fought against unions.

This early skepticism toward leftist ideology was strengthened by her 1936 experience, brief though it was, in Spain during the civil war. Her theoretical forays into politics might have prepared her somewhat for what she observed in the blood-drenched area near Saragossa and among the loyalist cadres of Barcelona. In that conceptual work, she realized the limits of an abstract approach to the everyday reality, hence her decision to work in factories, to go to war, to learn by doing. She was never under the illusion, however, that someone of her background and experience could really lose her privileged position in society, disappearing into the "working class." Nor was she interested in giving up her increasing influence as a political essayist – at least in the interests of any secular purpose. What she felt was important was to keep a record of her factory work and her military experiences and to tell the world what she had learned from them. She knew that without such experiences she would be tempted to both arrogance and ignorance – clever with words but unaware of social and political actuality.

Simone Weil went to Spain to talk with Communists and Socialists and with anarchists, whose particular cause she favored, to learn how those "causes," whose ideological premises she had already scrutinized, made their concrete appearance in civil war. Here was a seemingly clear-cut confrontation between good and evil: on the one hand a fascist military, a small and selfish landed gentry, a badly corrupted clergy, for centuries in the pockets of kings and queens, generals, and aristocratic owners of enormous estates; on the other hand, the republican forces, which, for all their political disarray, claimed to represent the interests of the peasants and workers, an impoverished people finally on the brink of political assertion through the democratic government that had replaced the monarchy. Though an accident removed her from the immediacy of combat, she had already made important observations. She had learned to be horrified not only by the murderousness of the Falangists, but by a similar kind of callousness in the people whose high ideals she herself espoused. How was this possible? She dared ask the kind of question that, once it is honestly asked, starts a person down a political road that can be unsettling and lonely. She kept up her inquiry and looked for company, a sign from anyone, no matter his or her loyalties, that her suspicions were not cranky, the disenchantment that comes from wildly unrealistic ideals.

In 1938 she came across *Les Grands cimetières sous la lune* by the novelist and political essayist Georges Bernanos, who had also been taking a close look at the same Spanish civil war. He had come to that war from the traditional "right," even "far right." He was a Royalist, a one-time member of Action Française, a group founded by Charles Maurras, who had been denounced as "fascist" for years, even by moderate French conservatives. He was also an accomplished storyteller, and his *Diary of a Country Priest* showed a Catholic sensibility at pains to acknowledge the central importance of Christ's pastoral life, his choosing to live among the poor, trying to feed them and heal them. The curé in that novel is a humble and sickly soul who lives obscurely, dies a painful, early death, and knows the frustrations that go with ministering to the down-and-out peasantry and their offspring. But he is also a bravely caring soul who fights cynicism stubbornly and resists every chance he gets to shift his loyalties, through the intricate mental rationalizations that make this possible, to the well-to-do, the socially prominent. He never becomes disdainful of the stiff-necked farmers who are not graceful or elegant in their words, their manners, and their way of treating one another.

It was this Bernanos[3] whom Simone Weil had already much admired: "The *Journal d'un curé de campagne* is in my opinion the best of them [his books], at least those I have read, and really a great book." But *Les Grands cimetières sous la lune* was the occasion for her to feel not only admiration, but genuine and strongly felt gratitude. "This last one, however, is a different matter," she wrote him in a letter that would become famous. "I have had an experience which corresponds to yours," she continued, "although it was much shorter and was less profound; and although it was apparently — but only apparently — embraced in a different spirit."[4]

They came from opposite political points of view to a common ground, a shared horror and outrage at the manner in which political aims are allowed, by those who militantly espouse them, to justify all imaginable crimes. Before she joins ranks with Bernanos and tells what she saw to be so awful, so monstrous, she offers that well-known novelist her own story, a brief but luminous political autobiography.

From my childhood onwards I sympathized with those organizations which spring from the lowest and least regarded social strata, until the time when I realized that such organizations are

of a kind to discourage all sympathy. The last in which I felt
some confidence was the Spanish CNT. I had traveled a little in
Spain before the Civil War, only a little, but enough to feel the
affection which it is hard not to feel for the Spanish people.
I had seen the anarchist movement as the natural expression of
that people's greatness and of its flaws, of its worthiest aspirations and of its unworthiest. The CNT and FAI were an
extraordinary mixture, to which anybody at all was admitted
and in which, consequently, one found immorality, cynicism,
fanaticism and cruelty, but also love and fraternal spirit and,
above all, that concern for honor which is so beautiful in the
humiliated. It seemed to one that the idealists preponderated
over the elements of violence and disorder.

Those are the words of someone who did not go to a war with
blinkers on, as may well have been the initial case with Bernanos.
Here was someone who had always wanted to be a pacifist – only
when Hitler violated the Munich arrangements with Chamberlain
and Daladier and brazenly marched into Prague did she throw
aside her ideological pacifism in favor of a resolution to fight
Nazism directly. Here was someone whose pacifism was not naive,
however. She had no illusions about the capacity of her chosen
compatriots to be mean-spirited, even given to "cruelty." This was
emphatically *not* an ex post facto realization, as was the case for
a number of Loyalist supporters who had the decency and political
courage to admit what they had learned at first hand: the corruption
of so many ethical principles; the gradual or precipitously abrupt
descent into evil (murder, rape, deceit) on the part of those who
proclaimed high egalitarian purposes and ideals. Orwell, for one,
was frank to tell us, in *Homage to Catalonia*, what his 1937
experience with those same Spanish anarchists had taught him.[5]
Like Simone Weil, Orwell saw redeeming virtues in the ordinary
people he met. (He was uncannily prophetic about what would
happen after Franco: the collapse of state fascism as a consequence
of its inability to "take" in a people with the cultural characteristics
of the Spanish.) But he broke decisively with "the political life"

as a result of his war experiences in Spain, and *Animal Farm* and *1984* state what Simone Weil had already written about before the Spanish civil war started.

In her letter to Bernanos, Simone Weil recalls the experiences which disillusioned her with vivid particularity and suggestive power. "I recognize the smell of civil war, the smell of blood and terror, which exhales from your book," she tells Bernanos, and then she mentions that she "was very nearly present at the execution of a priest." She explains the outcome. "In the minutes of suspense I was asking myself whether I should simply look on or whether I should try to intervene and get myself shot as well. I still don't know which I would have done if a lucky chance had not prevented the execution." She goes on, telling of a fifteen-year-old boy who was caught, given the choice of changing his loyalties, and when he refused, shot summarily. She tells of "revenge operations," of people caught ("haggard, terrified, famished creatures") and shot, of priests killed – and the surprise of those who witnessed such atrocities at her refusal to "laugh," when told the story! "One sets out as a volunteer, with the idea of sacrifice, and finds oneself in a war which resembles a war of mercenaries, only with much more cruelty and with less respect for the enemy."

She stops to continue her political autobiography, emphasizes that her kind of struggle is one for "the public good," for "the welfare of man." But these are generalities, she knows, and their espousal has to be tested not by pietistic words, and not even by detailed principles upon which programs would be based, but by an accounting of deeds. "In a country where the great majority of the poor are peasants the essential aim of every extreme-left party should be an improvement of the peasants' conditions; and perhaps the main issue of this war, at the beginning, was the redistribution of the land. But those peasants of Aragon, so poor and so splendid in the pride they have cherished through all their humiliations – one cannot say that they were even an object of curiosity to the militiamen." She refers, a bit further along, to "an abyss" which she observed "between the armed forces [on the Loyalist side] and the civilian population" and compares it to the similar one that

71

exists "between the rich and the poor." Then, this devastating comment: "One felt [the abyss] in the attitude of the two groups, the one always rather humble, submissive and timid, the other confident, off-hand and condescending." The letter ends on a tragic note – her sense that Bernanos, supposedly writing from a political direction of which she strongly disapproves, has ended up becoming "incomparably nearer" to her than the "comrades of the Aragon militias," those soldiers whose ranks she so urgently once wished to join; then she adds, "and yet I love them."

Her letter to Bernanos was written five years before she died. It did not represent a break with her politics. She wrote, still, from "the left," even though she saw in its "condescending" ways a source of difficulty. Her use of that word expressed the difference between her kind of "class analysis" and the Marxist kind. Marx could see, readily, the class position of leftist intellectuals, but he abstained from drawing the kind of political conclusions such a line of reasoning required. In a luminous essay written in 1943, "Is There a Marxist Doctrine?" which was at once appreciative and thoroughly critical of Marx's contribution to political thought, she points out, "Thus in the end Marx fell back into that group morality which revolted him to the point of making him hate society. Like the feudal magnates of old, like the businessmen of his own day, he had built for himself a morality which placed above good and evil the activity of the social group to which he belonged, that of professional revolutionaries."

The man who had studied so intensely and shrewdly the manner in which social forces coerce people, make liars or frauds out of them, and strip them of their dignity had somehow persuaded himself, despite all these past lessons, to allow one group an exemption from this seemingly inevitable development. Social lies are everywhere, but the "professional revolutionaries" will steer their way knowingly to social and political truth. He, who had analyzed the deceptions of the bourgeois state – and the way a large mass of human beings can be a weak and malleable force in the hands of others – had concluded, nevertheless, that their collective weakness, for the first time in history, would not be a serious temptation for those professional revolutionaries.

This terrible error is not an occasion for Simone Weil to turn against the Marxist dialectic. She still appreciated the value of vigorous theory, even in 1943, just before her death, when the strength of her mystical religious side was mighty, a threat to her very life. At the same time she remained alert to social and political mystifications. Why, she asked, hadn't Marx asked himself the obvious questions: How could *any* group transcend the human limitations all history has emphasized as universal, and what political circumstances would encourage such a group, or indeed, anyone in a given society, to have at least a fighting chance of such transcendence?

To her, as she read Marx and other social or political theorists on the left, such a lapse was no accident. She saw a snare at work: political thinkers and the professional revolutionaries whose contemporary or future activities they describe and justify are both trapped by their own willful illusions about human nature. Behind this delusion she saw a persisting political "materialism" that would never disappear this side of heaven. She recognized a human tendency built into the structure of collective life: our inherent capacity for taking advantage of one another, fueled by egoism.

Everything she saw about twentieth-century life only encouraged her moral guardedness, if not pessimism. In the last months of her life she had stopped to take the measure of her contemporaries, and her appraisal was grim. She saw most of us as more alone and cut off than we care to realize, no longer connected in time and space to a coherent cultural and political tradition. Some would insist that she was overstating the rootlessness of Westerners who live in advanced capitalist societies. But even now, over forty years later, a critical body of thought[6] emphasizes that rootlessness and the resulting self-centeredness that creates vulnerability to slogans and enticements. Her concern about the power propaganda can wield would have been heightened by the current media.

73

Simone Weil saw the modern state as the single most influential presence in the lives of rootless people, a virtually religious presence, because it commands enormous, dependent loyalty and, in the hands of certain charismatic leaders, a degree of compliance that can make millions seem servile. Given such a political reality, it would be fatuous, she believed, for leftist theorists to assume that a group of professional revolutionaries wouldn't end up grinding ordinary people down further, rather than struggling actively on their behalf. Nevertheless, she is grateful to Marx for his "truly great idea," his proclaimed realization that "in human society as well as in nature nothing takes place otherwise than through material transformations." Calling upon Marx, she reflects that "to desire is nothing. . . . We have got to know the material conditions which determine our possibilities of action." The person who wrote those words was, of course, not yet the one who turned to transcendent "possibilities of action." For her, desire — a union with God — would eventually become not nothing, but everything.

Her "critique of Marxism,"[7] is prophetically autobiographical. She sees Marx caught in a major contradiction. "This is what always happens," she warns, "the type of moral failing that we most fear and hate, that fills us with the greatest horror, is invariably the one into which we fall." She herself would struggle with this dilemma, comprehend the importance of "material transformations," yet convince herself, perhaps, that she could elude them and achieve a meeting with God while still very much a mortal. It is this Simone Weil, the critic appreciative of Marx yet able to see his blind spot, who refers cannily to his "quasi-mystical expressions," such as "the historic mission of the proletariat." She was not at all surprised that a "cult" of Marx had been made by "the Russian oppressors of our time." A historical analysis meant to be profoundly political and economic had become evangelical, a shift which could be seen later in her own journals.

The Need for Roots is a radiant moment in her writing. An extended essay in political sociology, its premises are precisely what, a half century later, many of us claim to have discovered about ourselves. She spotted the loss of familiarity, if not of family itself, which makes us so eager to invest a political figure with qualities that mitigate our loneliness and confusion and nourish our desperate striving for moral coherence. She spotted, too, how the self becomes our last refuge, the solipsistic withdrawal common to many who have material possessions and good social standing and whose indifference to politics ("I never bother to vote – what difference does it make?") makes our lives all the more political: a "force" with which the various individuals who *do* care about politics will most certainly reckon. The intensity of her social comments on our rootlessness, and the space she gave the matter, reflected her awareness that the concepts such as "mass-man," and "estrangement," then common in philosophical discourse, also had enormous political significance. Her mind's capacity to be comfortable with the paradoxical allowed Simone Weil a vision of the ordinary working person as profound as her vision of Marx. She saw how we often succumb to that which we most explicitly claim to renounce. Self-centeredness, wantonly encouraged by a culture for craven economic reasons, can turn overnight into a massive group immersion in political drama: the leader a pied piper who has, at last, called all the desperately private souls into the public arena for his own purposes.

There is no question that the spectacle of Hitler, Stalin, Mussolini, and Franco sharpened the cautionary side of her political thinking. She was a subtle enough psychological observer to realize the reasons dictators appeal to people, but she did not feel that people inevitably became social or political automatons. For her, a desirable politics meant an activity which truly engaged all citizens, setting their hearts, minds, and souls vigorously in pursuit of the ethically evident. To vote or not to vote, to belong to this party or that one, were for her meaningless alternatives: their very prevalence as important questions were a measure of how degraded a nation's political life has become. She saw politics, as did her ancient Greek mentors, as a noble pursuit meant for everyone, a means of finding coherence and living out one's virtuous possibilities. She had little of the scorn for everyday local politics characteristic of some academic or intellectual people. Nor was she impressed with the universalist political ethic of those she knew on the left – the whole world their country, mankind their people. She was convinced that people are meant to know and work intimately with their neighbors and that when they are unable to do so, when they leave home for a job that makes them impersonal stiffs, connected to no one in particular, simply the owners of cards that are punched twice daily, then they have lost enough dignity to make them a political threat, ready for false promises.

The report she wrote for the exiled de Gaulle government stressed the importance of a newly energized patriotism. Suddenly, amid disaster, the French people had begun to realize how much their nation meant to them, how much they treasured all the small details of existence whose everyday execution required a stable national life. The Nazis had struck at the heart of that life, robbing a country of its character. Amidst the great sadness arose a realization of how much had been taken for granted. For Simone Weil, the great challenge awaiting France was how to keep alive the heightened national pride and affection that defeat had inspired. She did not have in mind the crude militarism and chauvinism that wars stir up not only in soldiers but in almost everyone, including children. Her constant criticism of Rome fueled her suspicion of such nationalism, even though she knew the heady consequences, the tonic of slogans and parades. Instead she sought a kind of patriotism that would enable a nation's various social and economic constituencies to live side by side in a spirit of camaraderie and cooperative effort.

This vision, though utopian, was grounded in her experience in factory and farm work. When she went to work at the Alsthom Electrical Works, at the Forges de Basse-Indre in Boulogne-Billancourt, or as a field hand in Ardèche, or later as a government-sponsored writer and thinker, she saw herself fulfilling her responsibilities to a nation she loved. These feelings were not sentimental, or the glib "love of country" that makes people sing the national anthem and salute the flag in rote fashion. Her passion for French history and civilization, the language itself, and her obvious affection for those who spoke it, nurtured much of her working life. As a teacher she wanted her students to become French in a committed way. The beginning of the end for her may well have been her 1942 departure from French soil. She yearned for a return more avidly than many who were in exile, with an ardor for *la patrie* that she wanted to share with others.

She knew the risks. She warned repeatedly of the smug nationalism of certain rightist figures, Charles Maurras of Action Française, for example. Devotion to the nation can be at the expense of other nations and require contempt for those nations. "A terrible responsibility rests with us," she said in her long essay "Uprootedness." "For it is nothing less than a question of refashioning the soul of the country, and the temptation is so strong to do this by resorting to lies or half lies that it requires more than ordinary heroism to remain faithful to the truth."

This critical patriotism, this love of country that insists on continual reform, distanced her from both right and left. The former wanted a monarchist revival or a resurgent French empire, a patriotism for industrialists and generals that kept working people in their place. The latter wanted an aggressive "imperialism," she claimed, of the Stalinist kind, with expropriation of land, property, institutions, and canceling the freedom of neighboring countries all justified as part of history: the triumph of the "proletariat" over "reactionary forces." She was so saddened and outraged by the activities of the various political parties in the Third Republic that she advocated, as an "immediate, practical solution" for postwar France, no less than "the abolition of political parties." Of course, she knew and immediately pointed out that "the single party" would be "the worst end of all." But she persists. "The only remaining possibility is a public life without parties." She anticipates a certain skepticism, incredulity:

Nowadays, such an idea strikes us as a novel and daring proposition. All the better, since something novel is what is wanted. But, in point of fact, it is only going back to the tradition of 1789. In the eyes of the people of 1789, there was literally no other possibility. A public life like ours has been over the

77

course of the last half century would have seemed to them a hideous nightmare. They would never have believed it possible that a representative of the people should so divest himself of all personal dignity, as to allow himself to become the docile member of a party.

She follows that line of thought further, overstating her case dramatically. "Actually, at the present time, wherever there are political parties, democracy is dead." She pulls back a bit, acknowledging that "the parties in England have a certain tradition, spirit, function," which make them special, and that "the rival teams in the United States are not political parties." What they are in America, she doesn't say; nor does she mention the political parties of Sweden or Norway or Denmark, of Canada, Australia, or New Zealand, of Holland or Belgium. She advocates instead of parties various "associations," which have restricted and specific purposes—for instance, an association of workers which aims to defend their economic interests. But she is afraid of associations that become ideological, to the point that, unbelievably, she asserts that "the associations should not be allowed to have anything to do with ideas"![8]

She would reserve "ideas" for individuals, but she doesn't tell us what sorts of individuals would be charged with approving or disapproving of particular associations. She is writing a futuristic political scheme, a fantasy, a novel, as it were, of ideas. "As for the political parties," she says at one point, "if they were all strictly prohibited in a general atmosphere of liberty, it is to be hoped their underground existence would at any rate be made difficult for them." By whom? In "The Needs of the Soul," she uses the word *repression* without apparent embarrassment, declaring that it "could be exercised against the press, radio broadcasts, or anything else of a similar kind, not only for offenses against moral principles publicly recognized, but also for baseness of tone and thought, bad taste, vulgarity, or a subtly corrupting moral atmosphere." Then the following sentence: "This sort of repression could take place without in any way infringing on freedom of opinion." She gets specific.

78

For instance, a newspaper could be suppressed without the members of its editorial staff losing the right to go on publishing wherever they liked, or even, in the less serious cases, remain associated to carry on the same paper under another name. Only, it would have been publicly branded with infamy and would run the risk of being so again. Freedom of opinion can be claimed solely – and even then with certain reservations – by the journalist not by the paper; for it is only the journalist who is capable of forming an opinion.[9]

I quote the above at length to indicate how dangerously, if not ridiculously abstract she could become – how she brought the high principles of her life to bear on her notions of government. Here is an anarchist ready to blink at laws or regulations worthy of Hitler or Stalin. What prevented a mind so alert to inconsistency from asking itself the most simple of questions, namely, who, wielding what legal or constitutional authority, and with what policing authority, would implement the prohibitions she had proposed? Perhaps she was aware of her naiveté, hence her constant wish to test her ideas by working with others whose assumptions, desires, and difficulties were different from her own. (Not that her work in factories or on farms rid her political thought of this dogmatic and arbitrary side.)

She could be seen in the tradition of Rousseau and Plato, whom she mentions and admires, men of ideas who dared take on politics through writing. Plato's elites are Weil's, those whose decency, benevolence, and wisdom Weil keeps taking for granted in an uncharacteristic show of blind faith in human nature. Even as Rousseau wrote his proposals for a future Polish government, she kept writing on similar matters for the London government of General de Gaulle.

Sometimes she can exhibit a judicious, well-advised caution, as in this passage from her essay "Uprootedness": "Everything points to the fact that, unless supernatural grace intervenes, there is no form of cruelty or depravity of which ordinary, decent people are not capable, once the corresponding psychological mechanisms have been set in motion." In 1942–1943, she applies this skepticism to her beloved France's recent government:

> The Third Republic was another shock. It is easy to believe in
> national sovereignty so long as wicked kings or emperors hold
> the nation in thrall; people think if only they weren't there!
> . . . But when they *are* no longer there, when democracy
> has been installed and nevertheless the people are indubitably
> not sovereign, bewilderment is inevitable.

Yet, at another moment, she issues, almost casually, edicts such as "large factories should be abolished." She is dreaming, really, constructing a political sketch, utopian in nature, of "minute workshops scattered about everywhere," of "only a half a day's work" being required, so that "the rest of the time" would be given over to "hobnobbing with [fellow workers] similarly engaged." Like the late Huey Long, she wanted "every man a king," a kind of arbitrarily imposed populism far more coercive than anything he dreamed possible or desirable, though Roosevelt suspected Long of fascist leanings. For "every workman" she proposes "a house and a bit of land"; he would also own his part of the workshop, where he goes daily. "This triple proprietorship comprising machine, house, and land," she tells us, "would be bestowed on him by the State as a gift on his marriage, and provided he had successfully passed a difficult technical examination, accompanied by a test to check the level of his intelligence and general culture."

Who in "the State" would make these determinations? A stunning naiveté (or is it thoughtlessness?) is at work here, with the most obvious dangers around every corner. Didn't she see that the phrase "general culture" lends itself to the widest possible interpretations and could deteriorate quickly into a political means test? She, who knew the famous phrase L'état, c'est moi! somehow neglects to spell out the mechanisms which would control her utopian policies and programs. Even when she does get specific, she creates as many potential problems as she attempts to solve. "A workman unable to pass the technical examination," she informs us, "would remain in the position of a wage earner." She has established by fiat two classes, with the state's employees a hovering, shadowy third, though she offers this now lowly worker, literally a publicly defined failure, the chance "throughout the whole of his life, at whatever age, to make fresh attempts to satisfy the conditions." She will even give him "on several occasions" an opportunity "to be sent on a free course of some months at a training school." These men, by and large, "should be sent to fill jobs as manual laborers and pen-pushers, which are indispensable to the carrying on of the public services and trade." No matter that some of them might have talents, ideas, and energies which these proposed tests might not be able to evaluate. No matter that a state-administered division of property is to be established, with possibilities for friction that might make even the infamous Third Republic seem a paragon of common sense.

Like the dreamer Rousseau, she wrote about the lives of the young, and like him, she never reared children. (He fathered them, then abandoned them, and then dared tell parents how to bring them up.)[10] "During childhood," she instructs her readers, "enough time should be left out of school to enable children to spend many, many hours pottering about in their father's company while at work." She adds, "Semi-attendance at school – a few hours' study followed by a few hours' work – should then go on for some considerable time." She would encourage the child, eventually, to travel about France and see various kinds of working situations, and she would also offer membership in "youth associations of the *chantiers* or *compagnons* type." Each type mentioned, she well knew, had been sponsored by the Vichy government, both as educational camps *and* as a substitute for military service, which the German victors had banned. Again she grants the government, the state, astonishing leeway.

She takes pains to insist that the state will be "acting in the public interest" when, for instance, it accredits "the profession of manager," one of the higher functionaries. But as she moves higher up the ladder, there are always yet additional rungs to come: Who will accredit those who accredit, and so on? She is convinced that the "form of social existence" she has tried to plan for the late 1940s "would be neither Capitalist nor Socialist." Unfortunately the Vichy government had also made such a claim, a historic claim, of fascist movements. Simone Weil was not a Fascist, but she had in her an element of the didactic schoolteacher and a capacity to uphold the products of her speculative mind that blinded her to the dangers and traps in every paragraph of her programmatic romance.

But a close textual analysis of her political will and testament does not quite do justice to her political life. Though her political *thought* led her into the traps that threaten theorists – grandiosity, murkiness, disregard for the complexity of action – her political *life* still stands as a witness for well-to-do, well-educated Westerners who have wondered whether or how to become involved in the various social struggles of this century. She lived as the ancient Athenian social philosophers urged their fellow citizens to live, in constant readiness to immerse herself in one, then another national debate.

In the 1930s, when working people were engaged in repeated confrontations with those who managed and owned France's factories, she was quick to take their struggle to heart, to argue publicly and privately for what she believed to be right. Her essays were not the product of a literary careerist; she wrote from the heart as well as the head and in response to the urgencies of a particular political cause. Activism was a constant element in her life; she wanted to be in the thick of everyday discussion or argument. She dreamed that France would one day become a "city-state," as was Athens, and in that dream each French citizen would have the political passion she had, an eager and continuing interest in what is happening to the nation, a desire to join hands with others to solve whatever problems arise. She tested her dream daily as she walked the streets as a demonstrator, engaged in public discussion, and offered her energy as a volunteer.

Her effort to work in factories has prompted curiosity, admiration, and disdain in her readers. I do not think Simone Weil intended her factory work to be a political statement per se – the intellectual who renounces her class position in favor of the hardships of another, class-connected situation. Factory work, for her, was a means of exploring an aspect of French life then very much at the center of a political battle. She wanted to take a firsthand look so she could influence the outcome of that battle. She recognized that her experience was that of a temporary outsider, in a given situation voluntarily and briefly, as is so often the case when a relatively privileged person – George Orwell, James Agee again – makes such an inquiry.[11] She wasn't "slumming" in order to strengthen her credentials or to cleanse her soul and secure her honor. She was, rather, on an intensely political mission – to test as best she could her assumptions about the way people live and the way they might live as citizens of a country, as members of a community. She was also a dreamer.

"Conceivably a plant or factory could fill the soul through a powerful awareness by collective – one might well say, unanimous – life," she remarks. She elaborates with an interesting, stirring fantasy.

All noises have their meaning, they are all rhythmic, they fuse into a kind of giant respiration of the working collectivity in which it is exhilarating to play one's part. And because the sense of solitude is not touched, participation becomes even more exhilarating. Pursuing our hypothetical lead, there are only the metallic noises, the turning wheels, the bite of metal upon metal; noises that speak neither of nature nor of life, but of the serious, steady, uninterrupted acting of men upon things. Though lost in this great hum, one also dominates it; for over this permanent, yet ever-changing drone bass, what stands out while yet somehow fused with it, is the sound of one's machine. One does not feel insignificant as in a crowd, but indispensable. The transmission belts, supposing them to be present, allow the eye to drink in that unity of rhythm which the whole body feels through the sounds and the barely perceptible vibration of everything. Through the wan hours of winter mornings and evenings when only the electric lights are shining, all the senses are participants in a universe where nothing recalls nature, where nothing is gratuitous, where everything is sheer impact, the painful yet conquering impact of man upon matter. The lamps, the belts, the noise, the hard-cold iron-work, all converge toward the transmutation of man into workman.

This factory-dream, this poem, is reminiscent of the futurism that inspired artists, early in the twentieth century, to portray machinery as beautiful, redemptive. But then she cuts off her dream. "If factory life were really this, it would be only too beautiful. But such is, naturally, not the case." She concludes, a sentence or two later, that "[the factory workers] are not free." She refers to "the vise of their servitude" and describes it as a chronic state, which "grips them through the senses, their bodies, the thousand and one little details that crowd the minutes of which their lives are constituted."

She envisioned a nation made up of connected communities, with each of them rooted (how she loved that word) in important ways – by customs, habits, language, shared responsibilities, loyalties, and obligations. No question, this political dream had its weaknesses. But if we acknowledge the romantic side of her political vision, her foolish expectations with respect to what is possible in this world, we should also understand the motives and the point of view that gave shape to her ideas: a strongly compassionate response to the poor and a wish to see a world in which class resentments and privileges give way to an almost devotional respect of each for all, and of that "all" (the state) for each.

Over the brief span of her life there were significant shifts in her political interests and manner of thinking, though, to the end, her heart beat strong and loud for the world's humble and out-of-luck people. Her early Marxist-anarchist views gave way to a more structured notion of political life – an interest in hierarchical organization: levels of command and divisions of power in accordance with competence, achievement, and initiative. She respected property while refusing to grant it the sway it held in a capitalist world. She respected, increasingly, the state's authority, though she would have denied it the tight grip over millions held by the dictators who had plunged Europe into war. Words such as *organic* and *cooperative* and *syndicalist* have been correctly applied to her political vision, with its emphasis on both the individual and the various communities to which individuals belong, and in turn, the sum of those communities as an overall community, the nation. She was, in her own way, a nationalist – proudly French: eager to teach its history and learn from it, eager that French "rootedness" be encouraged and French politics be an expression of that rootedness. Others in Europe in the early 1940s were turning away from nationalism (as in the expression then common, "One World"), but she was a "communitarian"[12] and saw France, ultimately, as a community whose language, history, and traditions ought to be respected and transmitted with great care from generation to generation.

There was in her a strong yearning for the past which was at odds with her impatience toward the meanness and injustice that have come down through history. She never had the time to temper the rush of her political ideas with not only more personal experiences, but the kind of reflection which comes with living a long life and gaining distance on one's own dreams. Her politics was 1930s politics, and one must never forget that she died in the midst of a war which seemed, at the time, almost apocalyptic in nature: evil threatening to conquer the entire planet. In the face of the rise of Hitler and Stalin, of Mussolini and Franco, of the Japanese war lords, in the face of her own experience as an exile, as someone branded "Jew," she might have turned sour and gloomy in her politics, even as she was becoming increasingly frail in her health. But hers was, to the end, a politics of hope. She believed man was capable of responding to new social and cultural forms, to new economic policies, to a moral vision and a religious one which would transform the world.

I think the teacher in her predominated: throughout her life she was convinced that if only she and others like her could educate France's children, with respect to what mattered, then they, too, would become fervent idealists. In this lay her "calling," a calling she held with all her heart, and a calling she wanted to offer others:

85

politics as a vocation, as a means for individuals to go beyond their self-centeredness, to engage one another in the public arena, and for high social stakes. Maybe, deep down, her mind was drawn back to an ancient agora where it held conversations with Plato and Socrates, with Herodotus, with Aeschylus and Sophocles and Euripides, with Racine and Rousseau. But she never could forget her own century — the lives of humiliated men and women she had witnessed in the 1930s. Without question she wanted such people, also, to know those long-gone "friends" of hers and to have talks with them. Hers was, finally, a politics meant to give roots and ideals to a particular, beloved community, rather than build barricades of power and privilege.

Even in my worst moments I would not destroy a Greek statue or a fresco by Giotto. Why anything else then? Why, for example, a moment in the life of a human being who could have been happy for that moment?

Gravity and Grace

The "moral revival" which certain people wish to impose would be much worse than the condition it is meant to cure. If our present suffering ever leads to a revival, this will not be brought about through slogans but in silence and moral loneliness, through pain, misery, and terror, in the profoundest depths of each man's spirit.

On Science, Necessity and the
Love of God

Her Moral Loneliness

When Simone Weil met Trotsky, in late December of 1933, she argued with him, confronted him with what she saw to be the tyranny of the Soviet state over the Russian people, and sadly, heard him defend Stalin, his tormentor and ultimately his murderer. She knew a number of Socialists and Communists and no doubt in such encounters her mind began to distinguish between its political and moral imperatives. On the one hand, she was somewhat in awe of Trotsky and proud to have met him; she even received him in her parents' home. In her twenties, she associated eagerly and fearlessly with people like Trotsky and admired their interest in analyzing and advancing the historical struggle of poor and working-class people for economic and political power. On the other hand, she was beginning to distance herself from these tough, materialistic, strongly ideological friends — men and women in the labor movement and in the universities — whom she loved to meet and engage in lengthy conversation. Their assumptions about this life, she began to realize, were not the same as hers.

Trotsky, who had read some of her early political writing, was absolutely right when he called her an idealist; an intensely reflective person from childhood on, she was constantly trying to live in such a manner that her actions were in accord with her ideals. Already a moralist, she was her own first and most sternly addressed target of reproof. She needed no psychiatrist to tell her of the egoism she felt constantly at work within her, of her fierce pride, and of envy toward others gifted in various ways. Nor did she fail to notice, early on, that many who were most vocally on the left were living rather comfortably while proclaiming a solidarity with the workers. She was probably also aware that should any of those workers say or do anything that miffed these advocates of their cause, that crossed them in one way or another, they would be told off quickly and called a political name or two, as she herself would be: reactionary, bourgeois, all the familiar denunciations. (Trotsky called her those words, too.) For her such a pattern of behavior was terribly instructive – the mind at its self-serving and aggrandizing worst. She realized that such thinkers were cut off from their own moral life, because they were convinced their judgments were objective and historically correct. They saw themselves as liberated, immune to the seductions of middle-class morality and to that well-known opiate, that storehouse of illusions, religious thinking.

Simone Weil herself was not yet overtly preoccupied with religious thinking in the early 1930s, when her important writing first appeared, but unable to curb the moralist in herself, she was betraying signs of constant introspection. The moralist is already evident in "Reflections Concerning the Causes of Liberty and Social Oppression." This essay is one of the outstanding political documents of this century; Albert Camus praised it extravagantly,[1] comparing it to Marx's descriptive and analytic efforts, and so have others in Europe and the United States. I remember the late Perry Miller telling us in a seminar that it was a "stunning performance," and then he added that "the author was twenty-five when she finished the job" – meaning four or five years older than we, his students, then were. We read it as an elegantly argued social and political essay. Feeling another kind of urgency in the writing, I wrote a paper on "The Moral Voice of Simone Weil," trying to respond to the sadness and regret in the essay, the indignation and alarm. The young Simone Weil was not a scold or a preacher, but she was a moralist who had looked wide-eyed at Europe in the twentieth century and didn't like what she saw: "Never has the individual been so completely delivered up to a blind collectivity, and never have men been less capable, not only of subordinating their actions to their thoughts, but even of thinking."[2]

Even then she was sizing up "the Social Machine," a totalitarianism whose measure she had accurately taken – "a machine for breaking hearts and crushing spirits, a machine for manufacturing irresponsibility, stupidity, corruption, slackness, and, above all, dizziness." The word *dizziness* stands out – a puzzling, almost aesthetic word, seemingly anticlimactic, though the author would have it quite otherwise. She gives a clue to what she means with this observation: "We are living in a world in which nothing is made to man's measure; there exists a monstrous discrepancy between man's body, man's mind and the things which at the present time constitute the elements of human existence; everything is disequilibrium."

She was convinced that "the triumph of authoritarian and nationalist movements" had devastated millions of ordinary people, who had once placed their "hopes," as had she, "in democracy and in pacifism." But even though we now readily appreciate this obscure young student's early warning about such "movements," for which so many other intellectuals were rushing to find rationalizations, it is important to understand that what really mattered to her were the causes she mentioned in the title of her essay. The current moral and cultural malaise ran deep and wide and had existed, she was convinced, long before those three monsters of the 1930s, in Berlin, Rome, and Moscow, had made strutting self-presentations upon a stage of history, leaving it blood-soaked as never before.

As if to anticipate her literary as well as political critics, she makes sure, at the start, that she has prepared the reader for her much later use of the word *dizziness*. In a synoptic account of life in the industrial nations during the end of the Great Depression, she rivals Kierkegaard in *This Present Age*[3] and misses few failings of "contemporary social life":

Work is no longer done with the proud consciousness that one is being useful, but with the humiliating and agonizing feeling of enjoying a privilege bestowed by a temporary stroke of fortune, a privilege from which one excludes several human beings by the mere fact that one enjoys, in fact, a job. The leaders of industry themselves have lost that naive belief in unlimited economic progress which made them imagine that they had a mission. Technical progress seems to have gone bankrupt, since instead of happiness it has only brought the masses that physical and moral wretchedness in which we see them floundering; moreover, technical innovations are now banned everywhere, or very nearly so, except in industries connected with war. As for scientific progress, it is difficult to see what can be the use of piling up still more knowledge on to a heap already much too vast to be able to be embraced by the minds even of specialists; and experience has shown that our forefathers were mistaken in believing in the spread of enlightenment, since all that can be revealed to the masses is a miserable caricature of modern scientific culture, a caricature which, far from forming their judgment, accustoms them to be credulous, and itself suffers the backlash of the general confusion, which partly deprives it of its public, and by that very fact impairs inspiration. Finally, family life has become nothing but anxiety, now that society is closed to the young. The very generation for whom a feverish expectation of the future is the whole of life, vegetates, all over the world, with the feeling that it has no future, that there is no room for it in our world.

The foregoing excerpt is part of a yet longer introductory paragraph, above which she places a quotation from Spinoza ("With regard to human affairs, not to laugh, not to cry, not to become indignant, but to understand") and another from Marcus Aurelius ("The being gifted with reason can make every obstacle serve as material for his work, and turn it to account"). She goes on to admit, openly, her own dizziness: she simply can't "understand" without laughing and crying and becoming indignant. Nor is she altogether convinced that her powers of reasoning will really enable her to do justice in an essay to terrible "facts" which she can view only as unsettling in the extreme.

At the end of her long essay she uses an unforgettable phrase to describe what happens to someone who decides to scrutinize society so closely: to follow "such a course is to condemn oneself of a certainty to moral loneliness." She spells out what that "moral loneliness" means – that one won't be understood, that one will incur enemies all over, that those in positions of power – "servants of the existing order" – will be critical and punitive. The personal dimension of these words is clear; she foresaw the high costs of her own moral witness. The journey would be short, she believed, so all the more reason in her mind to persist in her reflections upon the badly faltering West, no matter the isolation she predicted for herself, and soon enough experienced.

As one reads her grave material and moral prognosis for the West, one is inclined, a half century later, to fault the essayist with unnecessary gloom. Her pessimistic prediction seems almost quaintly incorrect from the vantage point of the last years of the twentieth century. One wonders, though, whether Simone Weil, had she lived into a reasonably expectable old age – she would have been seventy-five, as I write these words – would have modified her moral analysis all that much. She mentions, at one point in her discussion of oppression that "a few moralists have perceived . . . [that] power contains a sort of fatality which weighs as pitilessly on those who command as on those who obey." She goes further, insisting that "it is in so far as it enslaves the former [the powerful] that, through their agency, it presses down upon the latter." Needless to mention, she was one of those "few moralists," utterly persuaded from the start of her career as a philosophy student that power – hence politics – is inescapably ironic, that fate strikes hardest at those who seem luckiest.

One suspects, therefore, that she would not be daunted by the survival and achievements of a world she saw to be in such imminent jeopardy, with the Nazi armies, seemingly invincible, headed everywhere at once, with scant opposition. Not only a moralist, but a moral historian, she was accustomed to the long view and its lessons: the Greeks at Troy, Rome's conquests and decline, the inquisitional church, Lenin's triumph and awful blindness. She might today want to revise some of her language, but one suspects she would still be our moral critic, our worried and apprehensive observer.

How accurately did she take the social and moral measure of things? If there is an element of distortion or amplification, if not hysterical exaggeration, in her account, is she a moralist in the negative sense of the word, with all its hectoring implications – the suggestion of self-righteousness, and yes, a touch of pleasure in the condemnation of others to this or that hell, be it secular or religious?

She saw her fellow factory workers in the 1930s as demoralized, reduced to automatons. It is hard to know how much time she spent in actual conversation with some of them. While she always watched the world around her, it was through the mediation of her own prejudices or biases; more neutrally put they would be called her point of view. As I read her "reflections," her long and somber and almost mournful look at the "social oppression" she saw everywhere – even among the wealthy and powerful – I thought of her successors today – Christopher Lasch, for example, who, with a sharp eye and a keen scent for this life's everyday cultural *merde*, has revealed to us our rampant self-preoccupations. For him it is also not an occasion of individual finger-pointing, but a historical view of things much like the one Simone Weil gave her French readers five decades ago.[4] Yet, even as I have found their arguments compelling and helpful, I have thought back to the men, women, and children I have come to know in the course of my work, and wondered about their narcissism. How inflated is it? How significantly has "the culture of narcissism" – our endless obsession with the self in the social sciences, in the cult of celebrity, in journalism and literature – affected millions of ordinary families? Lasch (and Weil) would be the first to consider these families more important in the moral scheme of things than the self-advertising ones whose self-involvements are loud and clear.

Perhaps such questions are the wrong ones to be asked of cultural essayists or moralists. Weil and Lasch are examining decades of the twentieth century with an extended, sweeping view; they are not doing detailed life histories. They are expressing their horror at what they see in whole nations, rather than setting out to collar a particular person. Still, at some point their analysis hinges on its applicability to the lives of individuals, on the resonance between analytic statement and the "human actuality" James Agee mentioned in *Let Us Now Praise Famous Men*. He, in contrast, struggled to focus his brilliantly knowing mind, able to comprehend the sociological, the cross-cultural, the regional, and the historical, upon "three tenant farmers."[5]

My hunch is that in the 1930s, as today, there were plenty of French men and women who would have described themselves as possessed of "proud consciousness" as they did their work; many "leaders of industry" who had not given up a "naive belief in unlimited economic progress"; and much "technical progress," with no evidence of bankruptcy. There was "scientific progress" of real potential value to many people, including research that soon would culminate in the discovery of antibiotics; forms of art that were vital, engaging, and suggestive; and a family life that ought not have been offhandedly described as having "become nothing but anxiety." I doubt that Weil ever meant to characterize her own family in these words. She had great respect for her father; she was genuinely attached to her affectionate and solicitous mother; and she admired her brother, even as she envied his marvelously acute, penetrating mind. Phrases such as "nothing but" turn out to be rhetorical, a writer's insistence on going for broke.

In her moral analysis, Simone Weil joins the company of Kierkegaard and Gabriel Marcel and Sartre, and as well, of her admirer Albert Camus: severe moral critics, whether religiously inspired or in a secular tradition. Orwell, too, of course – and he deserves special mention, because it is remarkable how precisely she anticipated his warning of the impact totalitarianism would have on the personal and public morality of ordinary men and women. Fifteen or so years before *Animal Farm* and *1984*, she had predicted what would happen "in the name of this utopia [for which] revolutionaries have shed their blood." She exposed the workings of political power, the whole "mad merry-go-round" of bluff and deceit and brutality with pitiless clarity: the never-ceasing "substitution of means for ends," rationalized by the most murderous of individuals in the name of practicality and *realpolitik*. What Orwell gives us in those postwar stories, written while he was dying of tuberculosis, she had rendered in a stunningly direct and logical line of analysis. Her prose became a powerful weapon against the "force" at work in the Kremlin and in the desecrated, rump Reichstag and in the rooms from which Il Duce strutted, to appear on the Piazza del Venezia, fat chin lifted high, comic daylight gestures a cover-up for many nights of torture and murder.

After all this despair she offers, in the next segment of the Reflections, a "theoretical picture of a free society." She starts it with a marvelous rhetorical statement, worthy of those late nineteenth-century documents which inspired us on this continent as well: "And yet nothing on earth can stop man from feeling himself born for liberty." He is, she insists, a "thinking creature," even when enslaved. "Perfect liberty is what we must try to represent to ourselves," this demanding writer says, and quickly adds, "not in the hope of attaining a less imperfect liberty than in our present condition," but because "one can only steer towards an ideal." Though she also acknowledges that "the ideal is just as unattainable as the dream," she points out that the ideal "differs from the dream in that it concerns reality."

She is engaged in the dialectic of the moralist. She is aware that what she calls "this pitiless universe" weighs upon us all the time, pushing and pulling at us in ways that remind us of the distance between abstract notions (the ideal) and the everyday "reality" which has to do with plain survival amid dozens of potential impasses. Yet those fearful challenges and dangers can make us stronger; they test us and give us the power to use the freedom we've earned: "A nation of idlers might well amuse itself by giving itself obstacles to overcome, exercise itself in the sciences, in the arts, in games; but the efforts that are the results of pure whim do not form for man a means of controlling his own whims."

Her definition of liberty – and ultimately of happiness – is not so much conceptual as exemplified by ordinary lives. For her, caprice continually indulged or money and power endlessly accumulated are two sides of a meaningless coin. Liberty and happiness are made possible by a certain kind of understanding. When, deep down, one feels in possession of that understanding, it creates "a relationship between thought and action." In an important elaboration of these ideas, she points out that "pain and failure can make a man unhappy, but cannot humiliate him as long as it is he himself who disposes of his own capacity for action."

She is smart about the world, aware that for millions and millions of people "the pressure exerted by necessity will never be relaxed for one single moment." Such people need no lecture from moralists on how "the good life" ought to be lived, no long discourse "on liberty," on the nature of "justice." Nor do they need to be told how "pitiless" this world is; indeed, their best hope, maybe even their last chance, morally, may be to escape that awareness. Simone Weil emphasizes a felt personal honor, a self-respect that may well be the most precious of all possessions, that which enables people, in her words, to know in their hearts "the contrast between servitude and liberty" and to feel nearer liberty. It was this awareness that often set her apart, this young moralist, pitting her frail body against so many imponderables and never settling for the delicious sanctuary that reason unconnected to reality can provide – the sanctuary of the mind dancing in the dark, while hundreds of millions lie in the heavy sleep that is all that separates them, day after day, from a "pitiless universe."

Her words once came back to me as I spoke with an American machine tool worker. He expressed what oppression and liberty have come to mean for him as he drives his car, does his work, falls asleep, and rises again, freshened and weary both.

97

"My father used to call himself a 'working stiff,' when he was real tired and everything was falling in on him, the debts and no job and my mother with her illness and he with his. But he got up, and when he didn't have a job, he kept looking for one, and when he did, he tried to keep it and work, 'work like a dog,' he always said, that's what he did.

"I think of him sometimes when my muscles are worn down to nothing, and I'm so thirsty I could drink a whole reservoir of water, and all I can see is my poor wife and that checkbook, and it's always *red* we're in, no matter how careful we are. I'm talking abut necessities, not your luxuries. I'm talking about food bills and clothing bills and the rest, and about doctors' bills and the dentist's bills. I have this life-insurance policy, and it's enough to make you cry: it'd be gone, all of it, so fast, after I died, that I'm sure someone would think to himself: Isn't that man worth more than *that*?

"Hell, you can't decide how much you're worth by the numbers on your insurance policy! . . . There will be a morning when I shave, I cut those whiskers, I scrub my face, I clean my damn teeth of the tobacco stains as best I can, and when I stop and catch a look at the 'me' that's behind the hair growing on my chin and my cheeks, and behind the teeth, and behind the face, and if I can say that 'me' inside my head isn't a bad guy, and he's trying to be as decent as he can, and he's trying to respect his wife and kids, and love them (and bring home the bacon to them!), and he's a 'failure,' maybe, compared to some, and he'll die pretty poor, but he can still look himself in the eye and say he's never really crossed the line into *bad*, he's tried as best he can to be *good*, and even with his scars and all, he's still plugging. Why, then if I can say all that, I have a right to give myself a wink and say go ahead, meet the day the best you can, and like my dad used to tell me, 'Hold your head high,' and if you can do that, no one's got that big a hold on you, no matter who he is."

It was Simone Weil's genius not only to formulate ideas, but demand that they reckon with lives such as that worker's – those of the overwhelming majority. For all the despair Simone Weil saw in those factories she saw glimpses, too, of human dignity – skilled workers proud of their capabilities and their daily achievements. At one point she speaks of "moderation and courage, virtues without which life is nothing but a disgraceful frenzy." She is convinced that "true liberty" would be found in the tool worker's life, in yours and mine, "if the material conditions that enable him [any of us] to exist were the work of his mind directing the effort of his muscles." Many of us, brought up to be aware of the unconscious as having its own demonic, belligerent side, will raise our eyebrows and wonder if any transformation of "material conditions" would bring about such a state of liberty for any of us. I heard the worker I quoted say as much, though not in psychoanalytic jargon.

> "I saw this man win a fat pile of dough on Megabucks [a state lottery] and I kept wondering to myself, Hey, fella, how'd you do if that happened to you – an oil well in your backyard, getting the green bills for twenty years, no matter what? I don't know what would happen to me. I might go nuts! I might go to pot, turn into a booze fiend and a lecher and a snotty rich guy who buys and buys, trying to show what a big deal he is, what he can do, and no one else he knows can, and how important he's become, saying to everyone out there, 'Just envy me!' Lord, I'd be a jerk, and God would tell me I'll pay for it later. Twenty years is a long time, but like they say in church, eternity is longer!"

With all that man's psychological realism, he has his dreams of a world that is better than any he is likely ever to see, as did Simone Weil. "If only a person could be himself more," he once said to my wife and me. Feeling the strong passion behind these words – and the anger at "officials, and more officials" and at "red tape" and at "people who have no principles, only selfish interests" – we immediately thought of Simone Weil. We thought, too, of the decentralization she hoped for, and her Orwellian assault on "the exploitation of stupidity and lies as means of propaganda" and "the mechanization of thought itself." She abhorred the "contempt of the individual" she saw in Germany and the Soviet Union, and alas, in the Western democracies as well, where psychologically mischievous and socially manipulative advertisers or experts in crowd behavior, even then, prefigured our contemporary media consultants, our contrived television politics: slogans, cleverly suggestive photos and scenes, lots of talking out of both sides of the mouth. She wanted each one of us to escape "the contagion of folly and collective frenzy by reaffirming on his [or her] own account, over the head of the social idol, the original pact between the mind and the universe."

In her rigorous analysis of history, from ancient Troy to her own times, Simone Weil saw force everywhere the great presence. Hence Marx's foolishness, she pointed out, his abdication of historical and psychological perspective, when he allowed for a secular moment of transcendence: that "dictatorship of the proletariat" which would eventually "wither away." She knew how unlikely, how absurd such a notion was. She knew, morally, what ought to be, but she knew as a slave, as a brilliant slave, how oppressive force is on anyone's life, and on society. People are slaves to consumerism or acquisitiveness, to pride and its trappings (offices, titles, prizes), to whatever appetite holds sway. In her own case, she once said, she ate not food, but words. "I only read what I am hungry for at the moment when I have an appetite for it, and then I do not read, I eat." No wonder she adds, immediately, "God in his mercy had prevented me from reading the mystics." If she had devoured those mystics, she realized, her force would yet again have shown its authority, with an article or essay the thoroughly unredemptive result!

Her moral search gave Simone Weil values and ideals which she announced in powerfully stated letters, journal fragments, published essays, classroom presentations, café discussions, and outlines on behalf of her country's future and the world's. The thrust of that moral analysis was always as gloomy and guarded as the word *slave* suggests. She knew how enslaved we all are to our passions, pride not the least of them, hence the bind of a moral life: it can have ideals, but their lasting implementation seems always beyond our grasp. However, her religious search would enable her to find a new energy and tone for that moral inquiry.

The marvelously astute but ultimately skeptical moralist who could take on a Marx, a Lenin, a Freud, the Spanish Loyalists, or the politicians of the Third Republic had by 1937 and 1938 (not yet thirty) worked herself into a corner stubbornly all her own. She understood everyone and everything, it seemed; her wide-ranging mind, which traveled easily through science, social science, the humanities, across cultures, historical eras, and philosophical schools, had enabled her to sort out her moral assumptions. These she tested through factory work and the trip to Spain's Loyalist army. Yet she was cranky, isolated. She intimidated any number of people, readers and those she met, by the force in her, intellectual and emotional both, a force which had become her personality, her self-presentation. Her utterly demanding, potentially scornful eye spotted all pretension, fear, reserve, hypocrisy, and uncertainty. What could anyone who met her do but surrender to this exhausting judge of all things, all people? She seemed in danger of becoming a slave to her own intellect, a lonely moral scourge whose magnificent capacity to dream of what ought to be was imprisoned by pessimism about what can be.

Then, of a sudden, God's arrival and entrance. Her moral sensibility may have been seeking a path of resolution, but as Simone Weil puts it, she as a person — as compared to her intellect — never embarked on a religious search. Rather, Jesus came. Now she was a happy slave, a slave with a future. At last she could begin to imagine that liberty — for her once the stuff of unfulfilled ideals and dreams — might be realized. But right away she began asking what this Christianity she found descending upon her meant, with respect to the way we live, the notion we have of the future, the agenda of existence. Her last spell on earth would find her enslaved to those questions.

Simone Weil's moral search was now shaped by the implications of what had befallen her. Matters of faith took on political and social ramifications. She knew the craving of people for direction, for institutions which in some way offer continuity, stability, and a sense of purpose. In the last year of her life, as she wrote what is now known as *The Need for Roots*, with its sketches of a postwar world, a France of her dreams, she not only used the metaphor of rootedness; she tried to spell out "the needs of the soul" if an undermining, disheartening uprootedness were not to develop. Her recitation of those needs amounts to a remarkable conservative manifesto, a powerful statement on her part with respect to politics and social institutions.[6] The categories are themselves instructive to consider — order, private property, honor, hierarchism, obedience. If there is equality, there is also liberty and freedom of opinion. If there is collective property, there is also not only private property but security, punishment, responsibility, and risk.

Among the needs she spells out one finds, early on, the beauty of the world, a certain rhythm and regularity which gives us the conviction that all is not random, accidental. The night does follow the day, and the day the night. The moon comes, goes, reappears. Stars are rather fixed in their paths, in our experience as watchers of the night. The seasons have their appearance and disappearance. All this is obvious, but her genius, always, was to connect the seemingly complex, the abstract, with the everyday, the common occurrences, as a novelist does. Her journals are full of such connections — the bounty she claimed as a result of her various and repeated forays into the world of workers, farm hands, students, soldiers, and people praying or trying to survive one or another individual and familial hurdle. She understood our daily passion for structure and predictability, no doubt to the irritation, if not outrage, of those who have made *destabilization* or *permanent revolution* buzzwords of our time.

Similarly, she refers to liberty ("the ability to choose") as second in importance to order — the requirement each of us has for our particular pathway. Next comes obedience, by which her readers may wonder if this is, really, the anarchist "red Virgin," or instead, an apologist for the *ancien régime*.

Obedience is a vital need of the human soul. It is of two kinds: obedience to established rules and obedience to human beings looked upon as leaders. It presupposes consent, not in regard to every single order received, but the kind of consent that is given once and for all, with the sole reservation, in case of need, that the demands of conscience be satisfied.

Of course, she is talking about obedience of a certain kind.

It requires to be recognized, and above all by leaders themselves, that consent and not fear of punishment or hope of reward constitutes, in fact, the mainspring of obedience, so that submission may never be mistaken for servility. It should also be realized that those who command, obey in their turn, and the whole hierarchy should have its face set in the direction of a goal whose importance and even grandeur can be felt by all, from the highest to the lowest.

Once more the utopian – she hopes for a wholeness of vision, a shared sense of what matters, a mutual obligation between the so-called higher orders and those below them. She tried to use "higher" and "lower" in a nonpejorative manner, with those called leaders very much the equal of those called the led, and with those called leaders, as she indicated, constrained by *their* souls' hunger for obedience. In her section on equality she makes all that clear, struggling with matters which continue to vex us now, and which, no doubt, will vex us until the end of time itself. Who becomes a leader, and why? Who, given what opportunities, becomes a member of the led? She uses a phrase we have come to know well – "equality of opportunity" – hoping that some day in the France she loved it would be said that "the prospects are the same for every child." Still, she recognizes certain "inevitable differences" in people, though she wants them "never to imply any difference in the degree of respect [shown to others]."

In her section on hierarchism she continues the struggle, aware that not only are there various levels, but that we yearn to venerate

103

others, though that attitude should be reciprocated by those to whom we turn. She dreamed of mutual affection between individuals and groups of people and dares assert that the way we respond to others in whatever position we happen to occupy is a moral issue. She takes the risk of mentioning the symbolic side of life – with the superiors symbolizing "that realm situated high above all men and whose expression in this world is made up of the obligations owed each man to his fellow men." Clearly such a statement can be readily mocked as handy for any fascist tyrant's scheme of things. In only one terse paragraph does she actually write of hierarchism, and one wonders, had she lived, what she might have done with the subject. No doubt drawing upon her experience as an observer in the world, she pointed out that certain people become a bit larger than life, and the rest of us, through our admiration, through looking up to the person, can ourselves be enlarged morally and spiritually. She saw this need in politics as well: a nation's citizens ought to feel respect for its hierarchy, not to be confused with fear or a blind obedience or a gullible and smug complacency that calls itself patriotism and loyalty.

When she writes of honor and punishment, she shows herself at her most idiosyncratic and interesting. She compares the all too quick celebrity of certain (military, sports) heroes with the way we ignore, or fail to see, the heroes among us. "The sometimes incredible heroism displayed by miners or fishermen barely awakens an echo among miners or fishermen themselves." Such a remark gives the reader great pause. In this wonderfully shrewd and decent way, she tries to light our lives morally. A half century ago, sick and dying, she took the measure of the culture of narcissism, the exact measure of a secular world morally famished (talk about anorexia nervosa), yet unaware that such is the case, or unwilling to respond to the crisis on its own terms, preferring, instead, "substitute gratifications."

We reveal ourselves by what or whom we loathe as well as by those whom we applaud. She took sharp aim at those granted high

honor who pay no attention at all to others, or who do pay attention, using words such as *scum* or *bums*.

> Deprivation of honor attains its extreme degree with that
> total deprivation of respect reserved for certain categories of
> human beings. In France, this affects, under various forms,
> prostitutes, ex-convicts, police agents, and the subproletariat
> composed of colonial immigrants and natives. Categories of
> this kind ought not exist.

She doesn't tell us how to do away with such categories, but
her observations are still valid. Her compassion for immigrants
was, as always, prophetic, given the Algerian crisis to come a
decade later and that of the transitory workers two decades later.
In her list figure the traditional categories which elicit the sympathy
of so-called leftists, yet the presence of police agents reminds us,
again, of a thinker's bravely independent mind, willing to spot the
prejudices of the liberal intelligentsia as well as those of conservative critics. As for her statement that "crime alone should place
the individual who has committed it outside the social pale, and
punishment should bring him back again into it," it is the kind of
remark that sets her apart from other social critics. "Punishment
must be an honor," she urges. "It must not only wipe out the
stigma of the crime," she adds, "but must be regarded as a supple-
mentary form of education, compelling a higher devotion to the
public good."

How to accomplish this? Would she have posed the question,
had she lived longer? She was clearly headed in a new direction,
politically, trying to envision a nation in which people were tied
strongly to one another, though not in the old, exploitative ways.
She tried to see past the vindictive, vengeful aspects of the law,
protective of property and privileges.

> The discredit attaching to the police, the irresponsible conduct
> of the judiciary, the prison system, the permanent social stigma

cast upon ex-convicts, the scale of penalties, which provides a much harsher punishment for ten acts of petty larceny than for one rape or certain types of murder, and which even provides punishments for ordinary misfortune – all this makes it impossible for there to exist among us, in France, anything that deserves the name of punishment. For punishment, as for crimes, the relative degree of immunity should increase, not as you go up, but as you go down the social scale.

Here we see a fighting effort on Simone Weil's part to connect the value of punishment to other values, to address the responsibilities of those who are proper, respected, who give orders and take for granted the law's fairness.

The section "Freedom of Opinion" in this inventory of the soul's needs is as controversial a piece as Simone Weil ever wrote and proposes a more conservative argument than most publicly identified American or British or French conservatives would ever care to advocate. She wants to see banished the sleazier side of opinion in the interests of the moral principles she believes important. She seems to have absolutely none of the qualms so many civil libertarians have, that one person's pleasure is another person's crime or sin. Up to a point, she grants the need for "complete, unlimited freedom of expression for every sort of opinion, without the least restriction or reserve." But she regards much that is written or produced in plays as intended to influence what she calls "the conduct of life," and here she is almost shocking and unflinchingly resolute in her insistence that these acts (these opinions), meant to affect the way people live, ought to be severely scrutinized.

She takes issue with André Gide's *Les Caves du Vatican*, with its evocation, if not celebration, of the gratuitous, the impulsive.[7] (Lafcadio, the hero, pushes a person off an Italian train simply to show himself able to do so – the purposeless act). "There is, then, no reason for placing such books behind the inviolable barrier of art for art's sake," she points out, whereas the law would require "sending to prison a young fellow who pushes somebody off a train in motion." She believes that "André Gide has always known that books like *Nourritures Terrestres* and *Les Caves du Vatican* have exercised an influence on the practical conduct of life of hundreds of young people, and he has been proud of that fact." She suggests that if a writer, thanks to the complete freedom of expression accorded him, publishes matter that goes contrary to the moral principles recognized by law, and if later on he becomes a notorious focus of influence, it is simple enough to ask him if he is prepared to state publicly that his writings do not express his personal attitude. If he is not prepared to do so, it is simple enough to punish him. If he lies, it is simple enough to discredit him. "Simple enough" is an easy phrase, but how does a nation safeguard freedoms while holding up moral principles? "Repression," she continues, "could be exercised against the press, radio broadcasts, or anything else of a similar kind, not only for offenses against moral principles publicly recognized, but also for baseness of tone and thought, bad taste, vulgarity, or a subtly corrupting moral atmosphere." After that startling recommendation we are offered a bit of whistling in the dark. "This sort of repression should take place without in any way infringing on freedom of opinion."

It can be argued that these were mere sketches, thoughts about France's postwar future set down on paper by a lonely exile, soon to die, during a terrible war, with painful memories of the decadence of the last years of the Third Republic. In this same section of *The Need for Roots* she advocates "the abolition of political parties," no doubt under the spell of similar dark memories of what the many and reckless and greedy parties did in France in the 1930s. (Her thinking, in this respect, was very similar to de Gaulle's and to the ideas held by the Free French in wartime London.) But instead of apologizing for her, through a psychological or historical, so-called contextual, explanation of why she said what, one may as well recognize her stern, reproving side, the streak of impatience that could turn into arbitrariness and self-righteousness. This went along with her strong devotion to certain moral principles; she detested the proudly amoral or value-free partisans of the liberal and radical intelligentsia. I think her social conservatism, her willingness to be punitive toward pornographers, toward various decadents, social and political, was an integral and persisting part of her, not some last-minute aberration as her health failed. In the section "Truth," the last of the soul's needs discussed ("The need of truth is more sacred than any other need"), she makes clear that these are deeply, sincerely held convictions.

> We all know that when journalism becomes indistinguishable from organized lying, it constitutes a crime. But we think it is a crime impossible to punish. What is there to stop the punishment of activities once they are recognized to be criminal ones? Where does this strange notion of nonpunishable crimes come from? It constitutes one of the most monstrous deformations of the judicial spirit.

Such extravagant excursions are not out of character. She had the boldest preferences or antagonisms and made any number of utterly foolish or unrealistic proposals, both radical and conservative. She wanted to dismantle large factories; establish tribunals to hector the likes of a Jacques Maritain[8] for not sharing her unqualified approval of the ancient Greeks; do away in large measure with labor unions. She dreamed of a house and some land for everyone, of a rather controlling state – ironically, one not unlike that of Vichy France during the Second World War. She, too, loved Marshal Pétain's *patria, familia*. Her preoccupation, if not obsession, with purity, with its strong sexual overtones, made her social and political thinking always susceptible to the prudishness in her personality. Nor was her radical side any less personal or impractical. There is an extremist direction to her moral and political compass – wild vacillations of direction that make the reader wonder what in the devil's name is going on.

But the more appropriate question might be: What in *God's* name was going on? Behind her lonely moral search, driving it, was another search, a spiritual one, which is extremist by definition. This underlying search may have been fulfilled at the end of her life. "It is impossible really to desire the good and not obtain it," she wrote in one of her notebooks. Her moral search had prepared her, and she was not one to cower before the implications her forthright mind had grasped.

Absolutely unmixed attention is prayer.

Love is not consolation, it is light.

Attachment is a manufacturer of illusions and whoever wants reality ought to be detached.

We must give up everything which is not grace and not even desire grace.

Gravity and Grace

Religion in so far as it is a source of consolation is a hindrance to true faith.

Notebooks

A Radical Grace

In her writing from 1933 to 1938, Simone Weil rarely used the word *God*. She referred to fate, to Providence, to the universe; she justified her moral search through recourse to history and through her strongly stated values, which she either simply assumed as worth espousing or summoned polemically as an inheritance from her beloved ancient Greeks, from certain French writers, and from social theorists such as Marx. During her last five years, however, her search became spiritual. In retrospect she maintained that this turn toward Christianity belonged to a lifelong sensibility. "I always adopted the Christian attitude as the only possible one. I might say I was born, I grew up, and I always remained within the Christian inspiration." These words are part of a letter, a "spiritual autobiography"[1] which she addressed, along with other religiously connected thoughts and concerns, to her beloved Father Perrin. This testimony tells of her early attraction for "the Christian conception in an explicit and rigorous manner, with the most specific notions it involves." She maintains that "some of these notions have been part of my outlook for as far back as I can remember."

It is hard to know whether that declaration is altogether accurate. Though the long letter is meant to be a confession, a chronicle of her search – or, she might prefer, her long wait – for God, it is also an arresting psychological document. Nowhere else does she become so personal, so willing to tell about moments of anguish. "At fourteen I fell into one of those fits of bottomless despair that came with adolescence, and I seriously thought of dying because of the mediocrity of my natural resources." She becomes even more precise. "The exceptional gifts of my brother, who had a childhood and youth comparable to those of Pascal, brought my own inferiority home to me."

Unlike Pascal, she and her brother did not lose their mother at an early age, nor was her brother a sickly child. Nor, one suspects, is the Pascal comparison intellectually valid, or so the brother would say.[2] Some of her remarks are prideful, melodramatic, even absurdly self-indulgent. "I did not mind having no visible successes, but what did grieve me was the idea of being excluded from that transcendent kingdom to which only the truly great have access and wherein truth abides. I preferred to die rather than live without that truth." It is interesting, actually, that she chooses this retrospective, confessional moment to remember such moments; they are in the Augustinian tradition of candid self-exposure, not at all flattering. She tells a bit further of her early love for Saint Francis of Assisi, her wish "that one day Fate would force upon" her no less than "the condition of a vagabond and a beggar." She adds that she "felt the same way about prison."

The dramatic side of her personality is evident in these remarks — the same quality that at the end of her life made her dream of a parachute descent upon the Continent. That wish, repeatedly stated to influential Free French officials, reveals someone quite willing to push life itself to its utmost limits. In the same spiritual autobiography she explicitly forecasts her own death: "And I am going [from Marseille to New York City, in 1942] more or less with the idea of probable death." When Anna Freud and I read that letter together, that sentence cried out for a response. I can remember Miss Freud shaking her head, a bit aghast, a bit puzzled, a bit sad. "She had begun to think of death before she contracted tuberculosis and probably not in connection with her eating problems, though I'm sure she had them at the time." She observed further,

I suppose if she had been telling us at the time what she wrote to the priest, we'd have wondered out loud what prison sentence she had in mind, for what crime! I find this more theatrical than substantive; I can't help wondering whether she wasn't being consciously self-dramatizing. If so, she had a long line of saints whose footsteps she may have wanted to follow!

We talked of Joan of Arc, of Teresa of Avila, of John of the Cross and the forceful way they took the stage to confront crusty, confining church officials or secular authorities. Miss Freud emphasized, without pejorative intent, this demonstrative side to religious life, as lived by those who take an active, charismatic part in it. Perhaps, she said, some of Weil's evocations of the past also had a theatrical element. "From my earliest childhood I always had also the Christian idea of love for one's neighbor, to which I gave the name of justice — a name it bears in many passages of the Gospel and which is so beautiful." Exactly how early in her childhood such thoughts occurred we are not told, but "earliest" in so precise a writer (her every word measured) no doubt means before fourteen, when her feelings, by her own description, toward one particular neighbor, her brother, were mixed. The point here is not psychological nitpicking but simply to highlight what can happen in a religious search: the perfectly natural posturing brought about by the intense desire to find goodness in one's life; the desire, also, to be worthy of a judgment no longer belonging to the self, but emanating from on high — a performance for God. She herself follows her declaration of early virtue with the following avowal:

> The idea of purity, with all that this work can imply for a Christian, took possession of me at the age of sixteen, after a period of several months during which I had been going through the emotional unrest natural in adolescence. This idea came to me when I was contemplating a mountain landscape and little by little it was imposed upon me in an irresistible manner.

She was known in her early 1930s Paris political days as the
red Virgin for her idiosyncratic mix of "purity" and left-leaning
politics. The most famous picture of her shows her wearing a large,
cloaklike coat, hiding all the contours of her body. She was dedicated to purity, to chastity, and is bold, candid, unashamed in her
repeated descriptions of herself as being approached, taken, cap-
tured by the Son of God. She believed that this happened during
one recitation of George Herbert's poem "Love," which she had
"learned by heart," and which she said over and over, often in the
midst of the "violent headaches" which plagued her. As she said
in a letter to Father Perrin, "Christ himself came down and took
possession of me." She insists that "in this sudden possession" of
her "by Christ" she had no initiative: "Neither my senses nor my
imagination had any part." She describes the consequence of the
visit in this manner: "I only felt in the midst of my suffering the
presence of a love, like that which one can read in the smile on a
beloved face."

This event took place in 1938 or 1939, as she approached
thirty. But in 1935, when she was twenty-six, she had already
begun to take an interest in religion, and it was then that the first
of "three contacts with Catholicism that really counted" took place.
After her stint of factory work, she had gone to Portugal with her
parents. She was exhausted, and she was having the migraine
headaches which had started when she was twelve and would
pursue her mercilessly throughout her adult life. When she worked
in the factories those headaches had been blinding, excruciatingly
painful. Other burdens had fallen on her as well. "As I worked in
the factory, indistinguishable to all eyes, including my own, from
the anonymous mass, the affliction of others entered into my flesh
and my soul." She claimed that these experiences changed her life.

What I went through there marked me in so lasting a manner
that still today [seven years later] when any human being
speaks to me without brutality, I cannot help having the impression that there must be a mistake and that unfortunately
the mistake will in all probability disappear. There I received

the mark of a slave, like the branding of the red-hot iron the
Romans put on the forehead of their most despised slaves.
Since then I have always regarded myself as a slave.

A slave of whom? And why — for what possible sins of omission
or commission? Noting the terrible suffering she experienced as a
factory worker — the lacerating pain of a severe, unrelenting migraine[3] — a psychiatrist might conclude that the phrase "branding
of the red-hot iron" applied to what she felt in her head; those
with migraine sometimes scour the language to find words
sufficiently strong to convey what they suffer. One patient told me
she felt, for days, as if her head were "a butcher block, and someone
out there with a sledgehammer was pounding it, pounding it, and
there wasn't a *me* left to say no, to say please don't, so all I could
do was take it, take it, and sometimes I wondered whether death
wouldn't be the sweetest thing possible." It is all too easy to reach
for a tidy explanation — such as migraine = anger and anxiety —
and ignore the particular response of this complex, extraordinary
woman.

In a seminar I once had on certain religious thinkers, including
Simone Weil, a student pressed me hard on her migraines and her
notion of herself as a slave; he wondered why I held back from
words like *masochism* and *aggression*, which gets "deflected," and
I had to admit (as I know Anna Freud would have admitted) that
I *wasn't* holding back from such words and all that they imply.
Such explanations come quickly to mind. But psychological explanations have a way of being all too static; they don't do justice to
the mind's lively, ever fluctuating rhythms. Diagnostic labels miss
the important question: What does *this* person, *that* person, end
up doing with a disease called migraine? What does she make of
it? Here is Simone Weil telling us where her particular misery led
her.

In this state of mind, then, and in a wretched condition physi-
cally, I entered the little Portuguese village, which, alas, was
very wretched too, on the very day of the festival of its patron

saint. It was the evening and there was a full moon over the sea. The wives of the fishermen were, in procession, making a tour of all the ships, carrying candles and singing what must certainly be very ancient hymns of a heartrending sadness. Nothing can give any idea of it. I have never heard anything so poignant unless it was the song of the boatmen on the Volga. There the conviction was suddenly borne in upon me that Christianity is pre-eminently the religion of slaves, that slaves cannot help belonging to it, and I among others.

She took her desperation to an obscure village and, so doing, went through a time of emotional ferment, of intellectual growth and change. Others with migraine have gone from doctor to doctor and clinic to clinic or from one treatment modality to another; they have tried travel, diversions at home, diets, medicines, and psychotherapy. Though she needed rest, she did not slow down and enjoy the scenery – Portugal's colorful and then quite isolated Atlantic coast. I suppose her response might be considered by some as itself a problem, a measure of her inability to relax, to enjoy life, to spare herself pain and anguish. But Kierkegaard might have thought differently. He might have noted Simone Weil's sense of "heartrending sadness" as a touching moment of moral empathy, as a refusal on her part to be the captive of aesthetics, of the contrived distractions sanctioned by society. He might have commented on the ethical energy at work. *This* migraine, for Kierkegaard, might have appeared catalytic rather than psychopathological, perhaps even evidence of grace.

Anna Freud related her reactions to a case presented to her in an English hospital. A nurse's aid had migraine and numerous fears, the result of an imaginative mental life that seemed to work overtime. The person presenting the case kept telling of the woman's "phobias," "psychosomatic" troubles ("a marked tendency to somatize"), and "primitive orality." Miss Freud didn't really disagree with any of the above formulations; she simply asked for "a little more," spelling out the request this way. "Each patient we see will take these serious troubles and do something different with them. We have to know not only what has been bothering this woman for all these years, but what she has done with her conflicts: what her life is like now, what she is interested in or tries to ignore completely, the story of her daily experiences." At the end of this "clinical case seminar," Miss Freud observed, gently, that "sometimes we have to wonder how a woman such as this, with all her burdens, manages to smile when she comes into the office, even if you and I know that the smile tells us of her nervousness and her much subdued anger."   !

In this light we might choose to marvel at the capacity of the young Simone Weil to turn her attention to those "wives of the fisherman," to call up in her thoughts that Russian folksong, to connect both of these with a religion, practiced in the everyday lives of people all over the world, the same people who attended Jesus a couple of thousand years ago. A twentieth-century French urban intellectual connects her heartrending sadness with that of obscure Portuguese villagers, with that of Russian oarsmen, and with the faith of the fishermen of Galilee.

During 1937, Simone Weil tells us, she had two "marvelous" days at Assisi. She describes this brief interlude tersely, but with suggestive, if not instructive language. "There [at Assisi], alone in the little twelfth-century Romanesque Chapel of Santa Maria degli Angeli, an incomparable marvel of purity where Saint Francis often used to pray, something stronger than I was compelled me for the first time to go down on my knees."

For a writer such as Simone Weil, the phrase "something stronger than I was" cannot help but be startling. Her own intellectual strength was considerable, no matter her protestations to the contrary (comparing herself to her brother). Her personality was also strong – a fiercely independent, willful, even eccentric nature. She exerted so much domination over so many of her impulses or urges that the words *discipline* and *self-control* hardly do justice to the reality of her daily life. She could do without sleep, without food. She spoke in a flat voice, which never rose to anger or irritation with others. She took as she wished from various writers, cultures, and historical eras and turned away, firmly, from what she found unappealing. She had no sex life. It is said that she cringed when touched. She cared little, it seemed, about clothes, and she took poor care, in general, of her body. Such behavior, obviously, appeased some voice in her, gave some autocrat dwelling within her cerebral hemispheres considerable satisfaction. How she managed to be "stronger" than all those impulses and cravings of her body, the rest of us who spend our lives both enjoying and resisting such impulses can never know. But now, for the first time, she declares herself "compelled" by "something stronger."

At last she was giving way rather than fighting off; she was yielding, saying yes, rather than stirring up a storm of heady discussion, then saying no. This was God's gift to a slave, whose usual master was the stronger part of her own mind. The consequence is described in the next paragraph.

In 1938, I spent ten days at Solesmes, from Palm Sunday to Easter Tuesday, following all the liturgical services. I was suffering from splitting headaches; each sound hurt me like a blow; by an extreme effort of concentration I was able to rise above this wretched flesh, to leave it to suffer by itself, heaped up in a corner, and to find a pure and perfect joy in the unimaginable beauty of the chanting and the words. This experience enabled me by analogy to get a better understanding of the possibility of a loving divine love in the midst of affliction. It goes without saying that in the course of these services the thought of the Passion of Christ entered into my head once and for all.

Now, at last, joy; now, at last, full sway to song, to love – "loving divine love." The change in her was radical. Right after the Passion of Christ entered her being, she noticed a young man. "There was a young English Catholic there from whom I gained my first idea of the supernatural power of the sacraments because of the truly angelic radiance with which he seemed to be clothed after going to communion." It was he who told her of the English metaphysical poets of the seventeenth century, he who introduced her not to love, but to George Herbert's "Love." She, who could refer to herself as a castaway object, as a reject, she who could "eat" words hungrily, yet let her flesh go untended, found "Love," found God, found joy. She also found release, now and then, from her headaches. A merciful God, many would say, need not come as such a surprise to anyone, need not overpower anyone, need not be the only passion of this life to the exclusion of food, sex, intimacy, and affection. But this slave did not, alas, know such a God.

Once Simone Weil met Christ, her life began anew, a slave, now, to a particular master. I think it fair to say that she fell in love with Jesus; that he became her beloved; that she kept him on her mind and in her heart. She spent the last five years of her life thinking about Jesus, writing about him, praying to him, fitting him into her social and economic and political scheme of things. She was a nun of sorts, following her vocation alone. She was an ambitious, dedicated follower, anxious to meet him — maybe become one of his saints.

She was a Roman Catholic in spirit, in faith. And yet her reluctance to be baptized is one of the better known facts of her life. Her letter to Father Perrin, dated January 19, 1942, and published well after her death as "Hesitations Concerning Baptism," a section of *Waiting for God*,[4] reveals her mind unmistakably at work: yet again that mix of ruthless logic and wild illogic; once more that harshness toward herself, the extreme seriousness that becomes, finally, both exhausting and comic. She seems to know that her correspondent is aware of this, is used to her mind's various strategies of obfuscation and radiant lucidity. She begins with a demurrer, no doubt seriously intentioned, though surely Father Perrin, her spiritual intimate, had by then become wryly amused by her self-critical apologies. "I am tired of talking to you about myself," she tells her priest, "for it is a wretched subject, but I am obliged to do so by the interest you take in me as a result of your charity."

The letter was persistently self-critical. Her central theme was that of spiritual inadequacy, which she is careful to describe as something other than a sly expression of humility on her part ("If

I possessed the virtue of humility, the most beautiful of all the virtues perhaps, I should not be in this miserable state of inadequacy"). She doesn't believe that she is capable of a "certain level of spirituality" – the devotion to the sacraments some Catholics feel. Her devotion, one comes to see, is directed at Christ, at his message, at his love and example, to the point that some theologians would emphasize her heretical Catholicism, if not her kinship with certain Protestant movements. "It seems to me that the will of God is that – I should not enter the Church at present. The reason for this I have told you already and it is still true. It is because the inhibition that holds me back is no less strongly to be felt in the moments of attention, love, and prayer than at other times." She reminds him that she wants desperately to stay in touch with "the immense and unfortunate multitude of unbelievers." She says, forthrightly and with no effort at false modesty, that she has "the essential need," indeed "the vocation," she puts it, "to move among men of every class and complexion, mixing with them and sharing their life and outlook, so far that is to say as conscience allows, merging into the crowd and disappearing among them, so that they show themselves as they are, putting off all disguises." She points out, after obviously considering the matter seriously, that she had decided against entering "a religious order," because she would, thereby, be separated "from ordinary people by a habit." True, she knows that some nuns are already separated from such ordinary people "by their natural purity of soul," but as for her, "I have the germ of all possible crimes, or nearly all, within me."

Her reluctance may have had other sources. She knew that she could have kept up her involvement with all sorts of people and still be baptized. Part of her actively and explicitly disliked the Church for its often dismal history. She was never one to forget, and not easily able to forgive, her faults or those of institutions, especially mighty ones. Though she knew Christ forgave the poor and the humble, to forgive the Church its long and sometimes sordid history (the Inquisition, the debauched papacy of the Middle Ages) was more than she could bring herself to do after years of careful study and contemplation.

In her New York notebooks, she went further than she apparently dared to go in her letter to the kindly Father Perrin. "The virtue of humility," she told herself in 1942, after writing to the priest, "is incompatible with the sense of belonging to a social group chosen by God, whether a nation (Hebrews, Romans, Germans, etc.) or a Church."[5] She asks herself, "How can the sacraments be rescued from a usurping social organization? By killing the dragon who guards the treasure?" She goes even further, abandons the indirection of a question. "The Church tries to use Paradise for blackmail and to damn anyone who rejects her infallibility. She will only become holy if she abdicates by renouncing her power to withhold the Sacraments." At one point she insists that "a new religion is needed." She doesn't spell out that revolutionary proposal, other than to specify "a Christianity so modified as to have become a different thing." Before using such words, she had been taking the church to task for its control over who gets absolution, and she had pointedly observed this. "If one is alone, shut up in one's room, one is heard by the Father who is in secret. If two or three are gathered together in the name of Christ, He is there. Apparently there ought not be more than three."

Yet Simone Weil could also write to Father Perrin these devotional statements.

I love God, Christ, and the Catholic faith as much as it is possible for so miserably inadequate a creature to love them. I love the saints through their writings and what is told of their lives — apart from some whom it is impossible for me to love fully or to consider saints. I love the six or seven Catholics of genuine spirituality whom chance has led me to meet in the course of my life. I love the Catholic liturgy, hymns, architecture, rites, and ceremonies. But I have not the slightest love for the Church in the strict sense of the word, apart from its relation to all these things that I do love.

She loved the Catholic faith, but the Church was another matter. I think she never forgave the Church for conquering the Roman empire. She considered herself a Catholic but, for her, to be a *Roman* Catholic meant to be intellectually provoked. Her contempt for Rome's empire was boundless, and she could find no saving irony in the triumph over that empire of a once obscure messianic movement in Palestine. On the other hand, for all her assaults on nationalism and consolidated power of various kinds, she was interested in power and wanted to see it used for the benefit of those in need. Like Orwell with respect to England, when the Second World War came she drew closer to political France (now an exiled, beaten institution, so more to her taste, which always ran to the humiliated, the downtrodden).

Even Georges Bernanos, a devoted Catholic and fiercely patriotic Frenchman, had misgivings similar to Simone Weil's. He shares her contempt for church officials and their power, their corrupted ways, in his *Diary of a Country Priest*. The curé who keeps a diary is not the only priest in the novel. Through him we meet others, and their pride or self-importance – the serious flaws of character the author chooses to evoke – is surely meant to remind us of the Church's suffering over the centuries at the hands of its own clergy. One thinks of Simone Weil especially at the very end of the novel, when the young curé, so good and decent and honest, so Christ-like, lies dying of stomach cancer. No longer are we reading his journal notes; he is almost gone. But a letter tells what happened just before his last breath was drawn.

> The priest was still on his way, and finally I was bound to voice my deep regret that such delay threatened to deprive my comrade of the final consolations of Our Church. He did not seem to hear me. But a few moments later he put his hand over mine, and his eyes entreated me to draw closer to him. He then uttered these words almost in my ear. And I am quite sure that I have recorded them accurately, for his voice, though halting, was strangely distinct.
> "Does it matter? Grace is everywhere . . ."
> I think he died just then.

There has been much discussion as to whether Simone Weil, at the very last moments of *her* life, received the Church's "consolations" – was finally baptized. She made such a fuss over the matter, worthy of the legalistic quibbling, alas, she condemned so vigorously in others. Indeed, the contrast between the curé Bernanos gives us and Simone Weil is instructive. "God might possibly wish my death as some form of example to others," the sick priest muses, "but I would rather have their pity. Why shouldn't I? I have loved them greatly, and I feel this world of living creatures has been pleasant. I cannot go without fears." As for the final words of his diary, one wishes they could have been there, big and bold, on the wall of her hospital room, as Simone Weil wasted away to the "nothingness" she so craved. "How easy it is to hate oneself! True grace is to forget. Yet if pride could die in us, the supreme grace would be to love oneself in all simplicity – as one would love any of those who themselves have suffered and loved in Christ."

This was not the Christianity of Simone Weil. She was kin to the suffering Christ. She was kin to a hungry God who sought souls from the infinity of space and time. For her the Crucifixion was the critical moment of all history. The last words of Jesus, a measure of His aloneness at the end – "My God, my God, why hast thou forsaken me?" – had enormous appeal to her; held her attention completely for long stretches of time; were for her evidence, through the spoken word, of a "state of perfection." She is obsessed with the psychology of the Cross – how it was that Jesus managed to rid himself of the pride, the self which the rest of us constantly cultivate, sometimes by denial. George Eliot's "unreflecting egoism," mentioned in *Middlemarch*[6] as a constant for all of us, was something Simone Weil sought to escape, but which she felt that only Jesus could transcend.

Still, she was persuaded that the badly oppressed, the down-and-out are at least existentially akin to Jesus in His last moments. But she also knew, shrewdly, that when such vulnerability is imposed by the world, and resented, rather than embraced wittingly and willingly, bitterness and vengefulness can result: "the apparently inexplicable vindictiveness of the fallen toward their benefactors." Here she was able, in her special way, to connect a complex theology to the social and political analysis she had sought to construct. She learned to distinguish between voluntary and imposed suffering and thereby spared herself the worst risks of her romantic nature, which had occasionally reached out to the poor as if their obvious concrete suffering translated into an equally concrete virtue. She learned, too, the distinction between spiritual poverty, which can be an affliction of the rich as well as the poor, and material poverty, which is an enforced, brutish imposition upon people.

In her early life as a political activist, she regarded poverty as a moral outrage: it is unconscionable, she felt, that some live extravagant lives while others clutch at scraps of food or grab at garbage, starve. Later, as she came to know the life of Jesus and reflected on how he spent his short time here – one year shorter than her life – she began to see poverty differently, as a means by which God chooses to instruct us. Simone Weil regarded Jesus as a fellow human being as well as God's son and was much interested in his personal struggle for perfection.[7] Jesus died in darkness and despair, not in a command post or the office of an important institution. His poverty was gladly assumed and almost enjoyed, not boastfully, but as the disciples enjoyed it in the course of their simple, everyday lives: he the carpenter, they the peasants, the fishermen. Simone Weil, with her factory work and farm work, her trek to Spain, her teaching, and her desire at the end to nurse Resistance fighters, to be parachuted into jeopardy – and camaraderie *in extremis* – was making, in sum, a statement of her radical Christianity. The condition of poverty to her was the essence of Christianity, an *assumed* situation of precariousness. At the same time, she recognized that poverty could also be demeaning, associated with terrible sins and wrongdoing of large proportions.

Plenty of Socialists or Communists have perceived what poverty does to poor people – the gravity of everyday slum life: hustling, conniving, callousness, malice. But the dream for the secular reformer is slum clearance and better schools and power to the people and doctors to treat ills and good food. The goal, as I once heard Herbert Marcuse put it, is a "transformation of behavior," Eros at last triumphant, in the form of an earthly "beloved community."

Simone Weil saw such a supposedly upward movement as more likely to be a downward one. She remembered other historical "victories" – for example, Christianity over Rome, and of course, Lenin and his cadres over the bourgeoisie. She was convinced that personal ambition always subverted such "progress," and that no secular strategy (laws, education, psychiatric treatment, to name a few of our favorite ones) would solve this problem. Cardinals of the Roman Catholic Church, popes, priests, prominent laymen, political activists whose bodies have been on the line for years, well-known and celebrated reformers, and much admired social theorists of liberation, of radical politics have all succumbed to pride, to selfishness. Come with me, follow the leader, and excuse my errors in the name of the future, in the name of the cause, the dialectic, the final breakthrough of this or that movement or historical initiative.

Simone Weil was averse to the seductions of theology and fought abstractions because she knew they tempted her. Instead, she turned toward Jesus, who did not seek power, who surrendered, who prayed for his enemies, endured the aloneness, the scorn of everyone, even the betrayal by a chosen friend. He was naked at the end, a word Simone Weil favored. To her this meant with no guises, rationalizations, self-justifications, plans, or programs; with no hope invested in a revolution or a counterrevolution, or even in the triumph one day of his ideas, if it meant a worldwide bureaucracy, a hierarchy with powerful, privileged figures.

Her anarchism influenced her view of Christianity. She was a radical Christian of the beggar and outcast variety, of the early Church variety: lucky to be alive today, tomorrow headed for a painful, desolate death, perhaps at the hands of a local despot, a contemptuous villager, or even a scared acquaintance or so-called friend. She distrusted success in any form, fearing an avalanche of eager, gullible "conversions." She looked anxiously for God's signals, meaning encouragement along the tough and wretched way of daily adherence to a harsh faith. "I come to bring you not peace but the sword." Above all, she feared the smothering hug of accommodation.

In this apocalyptic time, with Hitler and Stalin as anti-Christs, war and suffering and disorder and uncertainty prompted in less excitable sensibilities than hers a sense of gloom and doom. No wonder her Christianity was in harmony with that of the early Christians, who expected no comfort from religious or political authorities but only from the hovering presence of God.

She regarded God's very presence as a sacrifice. "For God to be born is renunciation. The birth of Christ is already a sacrifice. Christmas ought to be as sad a day as Good Friday." Her view is at such variance with conventional Christendom that the mind boggles on reading her diary entry.[8] She goes even further. "Every man, seeing himself from the point of view of God the Creator, should regard his own existence as a sacrifice made by God. I am God's abdication. The more I exist, the more God abdicates. So if I take God's side rather than my own I ought to regard my existence as a diminution, a decrease." She adds, after that startling explanation, this small comfort. "When anyone succeeds in doing this, Christ comes to dwell in his soul." As she had said earlier in a pithy summary that defies just about every secular twentieth-century value, "Salvation is consenting to die."

Such a salvation was sought by a woman I met in Rio in 1980. This woman lived high up a *favela*, within sight of the well-known statue of Jesus, which stands, with arms outstretched, on a mountain dominating the city.[9] She was in pain, dying of cancer at the age of thirty-one. She used to sit on a chair in the morning and stare at the statue of Jesus, stare so intently that no one could distract her. Once, as we talked, she explained this morning habit.

"I wake up and I think of God, far from here, very far. Yet, He visits us. He wants to see how 'they' are doing – us, His people. He knows we're bad. He knows all our sins. He knew them before He let us come here. He sent us here to give us a chance to love Him, to love each other, and then He'd love us. But we ruin the chance. I have. Everyone does. I know what people call 'love'! I've sold my body for years, until there was nothing left to sell! I became all used up, and now I'm ready to disappear. I weigh so little that a strong wind would carry me off. I wish a wind would come and do it – today!

"I sit and stare at Jesus, and beg Him to take me. I had a dream a while back that the wind came, and I was taken to the statue, and He smiled, and then I was taken right to Jesus, not the statue, and He was still smiling, and He told me I could spend all the time in the world sitting and watching the statue down below, and the people who pray to it, and the people who don't even notice it, and the people who laugh at it. The men I 'knew,' they asked me how I could think Jesus would have any use for me, because I'm so dirty, and He wants only the clean ones. Hah! Their wives are 'clean,' their rich wives, with their jewels and furs and big cars and the chauffeurs. Jesus sees their wives, and those men, and He cries for them, just like me. He cries for everyone – He cries too much! There are days when I've wanted Him to come here and kill and kill and kill, but He won't do it. The nuns try to explain to me why, but I know on my own: it's not in Him to be like that, a murderer!

"You ask how I know what He's like – well, I'll tell you. I sit and I pray to Him, and after a while, I know He's near me. He's ready to get me out of here, I'll think. But not yet, I find out! We have to stay here long enough to be ready to leave! I've been ready for a long time, but God is the One Who decides. I will wake up and my body is shaking, and the pain is every-where, and I can't breathe, and my feet are unable to hold me up, and every muscle is as tight as can be, and I'm bleeding, and I say, please, God, *enough*. I know He's waiting for me, only it's not yet the day. He must think I'm still too selfish! If only I could get rid of my crooked smile, the one I used for years to 'hook' men! My Copacabana smile. I'm near death, and I still have it!

"Last night I had a dream that I had died, at last! I was walk-ing to get water, and I dropped the can, and I started to fall down, and suddenly some hands came to my body, and I thought it was a man, and I was in a hotel room in the Copacabana, with one of them. But I wasn't. The hands lifted me up, and I was standing, and I looked around, but I couldn't see anyone. Where are my children? I wondered. But I could see no one. Then I was gone! I couldn't see myself, but I was there, and these hands were holding me, big hands, though I couldn't see them, either. I looked up to the sky, and that's when the cloud came down, and I was in the middle of the cloud, and I saw the face of Jesus, a big smile, and the sun shining in back of Him, and I was afraid, I was trembling. But He kept smiling, and I knew I was gone, from here; and then I woke up. I started crying!

"I went and sat and tried to plead with Jesus – the statue – to help me, to come and take me. But I have children here, and no man to help, and I'll live a little longer. I know how death comes now: hands you can't see lift you, and you don't fall, you just go toward Him, and He's ready to welcome you. He'll wash all the sores and the pain will stop. You're with Him, and that's the new life we're promised. I cry, thinking of it. I cry, thinking of the children I've lost. I cry from my body's troubles. I cry because we have nothing here, and my baby died a few years ago, because we had no doctor to save it, and we watched, and I waited for God to come and take the baby and He did. I was sure He was crying, too. He's always crying for us! That's His way!"

A long, rambling, feverish monologue. (She was *very* sick; the death she hoped for came a week later.) A woman of extreme poverty who had lived three decades of injury, loss, betrayal, hunger, sickness, and cruelty. She was beaten by men who loved to take their belts from their pants and go to work on her. As they did, she thought of Jesus, and hoped He forgave her, forgave them. ("They are nervous. They have lots of deals they're waiting to see work out, they tell me; and they don't sleep with their wives, not in the same bed.") Now, at the end, she gives expression to her yearning for Jesus, her continuing struggle, the gravity she, like Simone Weil, understands (the burden, the weight, of all this life's imperfections) and the grace she, like Simone Weil, hopes to receive. She was trying to leave behind her own egoism, to think of Jesus rather than herself, imagine his via dolorosa: all the suffering spread out, the world over. She was trying to pray for those men, pray for their wives, pray for all who exploit, even for all who exploit by being exploited.

"If I was a true Christian," she once told me, "I would let those men do what they want and refuse everything they offer, the money." Then she went on.

> "I would beg on the streets. I would sit and wait for Him to lift me up, and not move until He does! I should have become a nun! I should have never gone near a man! I should have offered to die for someone who needed to live more than me; I should have pleaded with Jesus to take me and let someone else stay a while longer — the woman over there who died: her six children have no one, and they will die soon. . . ."

"I'm waiting for Jesus to tell me it's my turn," she finally told me. The name Simone Weil crossed my mind, Simone Weil, waiting for God. I remember what the nuns told me about this woman, what one nun, in particular, said, having been approached by a perplexed and, frankly, alarmed pair of physicians, who recounted some of what they had heard and asked for help, an interpretation, perhaps.

> "She is a strange woman. She used to be very practical. She was almost coarsely practical! She told me once that she knew how the world worked, and she had no choice but to 'play the game,' according to what she would always tell us are 'the rules.' When I would ask her what the rules are, she would let me know so quickly that I realized each time how she was just waiting for me to get in her way, so she could get me out of her way! She was very determined; she let us know that she didn't expect anything from the world, and she didn't know how long

she would live, but while she was here, she would do all she could to keep her children alive and to teach them what the world has in store for them. I used to get bumps on my arms when I heard her talk like that; I felt she should be more gentle with herself and her children. But she knew what to say and do; *she* was living the life, not us. We are in another world, in this order. Jesus is protecting us, and He can't seem to protect her, and so many others like her.

"One afternoon she came to see me. I think she knew she was getting sick. She didn't come to find a doctor. She knew we could help her go to a clinic, but she was not one to take suggestions from others. She told me that she had a deck of cards, and she wanted to spread them before me! The next thing I knew she was doing just that – she was telling me what her situation was, and what she saw ahead. She had been given a bad hand by fate, and she could tell that she would soon be out of the game. She had been wondering *whose* game it is, this life. She had always gone to church, but she had never really taken it seriously, not the way she now thought ought to be the case. Not that it was *church* she wanted to take seriously. She was convinced that our church wasn't as 'pure' as some people in it. She had great respect for us nuns, she insisted, but she thought we have our heads buried in some Copacabana and Ipanema sand. I told her she was wrong, that we are no fools, and not nearly as innocent as she was sure we are. But she was not going to listen to me. She wanted me to listen to her. And I did.

"She said that Jesus is what is important, and if we want to be important, then there's only one way, by spending our lives, as much as possible, trying to be in touch with Him. The closer we get to Him, the better our chance for being saved, but He doesn't just save people the way they think He does: go to church and do what you're supposed to do. No, it's different. You have to become part of Him, she'll tell you! She's had a very active sexual life, and she thinks in those terms! I know her well, and she tells me what comes to her mind. I don't think she would talk about some of these matters with you! I'll be honest with you: when I have finished hearing her – the out-pouring of her mind! – I am dizzy. I am in – what is the word? – a swoon! I don't dare tell our Mother Superior! But I have a strange feeling that I have been brought closer to God, the real Jesus Who came to visit us!"

That "real Jesus" was for an obscure, impoverished Rio de Janeiro woman of questionable reputation, and for the nun who knew to admire her natural and even exalted religious sensibility, as well as for Simone Weil, a still electrifying, summoning presence. His words and deeds challenged the principalities and powers. Simone Weil knew, that *favelado* woman and that nun knew a radical Christianity in which "the last shall be first, and the first last," a radical Christianity which strikes hard at pride and the trappings of success, at self-importance and condescension toward fellow human beings. Their radical Christianity confronts all the sophisticated social and political and cultural institutions.

In similar spirit, Simone Weil wrote an extraordinary prayer in her notebook while she was in exile in New York.

Father, in the name of Christ, grant me this.

That I may be unable to will any bodily movement, or even any attempt at movement, like a total paralytic. That I may be incapable of receiving any sensation, like someone who is completely blind, deaf and deprived of all the senses. That I may be unable to make the slightest connection between two thoughts, even the simplest, like one of those total idiots who not only cannot count or read but have never even learnt to speak. That I may be insensible to every kind of grief and joy, and incapable of any love for any being or thing, and not even for myself, like old people in the last stage of decrepitude.

Father, in the name of Christ, grant me this in all reality.

May this body move or be still, with perfect suppleness or rigidity, in continuous conformity to thy will. May our faculties of hearing, sight, taste, smell and touch register the perfectly accurate impress of thy creation. May this mind, in fullest lucidity, connect all ideas in perfect conformity with thy truth. May this sensibility experience, in their greatest possible intensity and in all their purity, all the nuances of grief and joy. May this love be an absolutely devouring flame of love for God. May all this be stripped away from me, devoured by God, transformed into Christ's substance, and given for food to afflicted men whose body and soul lack every kind of nourishment. And let me be a paralytic – blind, deaf, witless and utterly decrepit.

Father, effect this transformation now, in the name of Christ; and although I ask it with imperfect faith, grant this request as if it were made with perfect faith.

Father, since thou art the Good, and I am mediocrity, rend this body and soul away from me to make them do things for your use, and let nothing remain of me, forever, except this rending itself, or else nothingness.[10]

She offers forthwith her own critique of what she has just written.

Words like this are not efficacious unless they are dictated by the spirit. One does not voluntarily ask for such things. One comes to it in spite of oneself. In spite of oneself, yet one comes to it. One does not consent to it with abandon, but with a violence exerted upon the entire soul by the entire soul. But the consent is total and unreserved, and given by a single movement of the whole being. Is it from this that the metaphor of marriage is taken? This relation between God and the soul resembles the relation between a bridegroom and a still virgin bride on their wedding night. Marriage is a consented rape. And so is the soul's union with God.

No question there is a historical tradition for *some* of the above – the mystical and ecstatic surrender of certain desert fathers and saints to pain, to God's beck and call.[11] In a course I teach with Robert Kiely at Harvard University, "The Literature of Christian Reflection," I hear my colleague discuss Juliana of Norwich, her petition to God for suffering, for a capacity to experience pain as almost delicious, and I think of Simone Weil. As I read about Saint Thérèse of Lisieux and the racking, gnawing belly pains she had to endure and the way she called out to the Lord in a hauntingly grateful acceptance of such a fate, I also think of Simone Weil.[12] A radical grace with all its demands had come to her, the grace of a God who had known terrible suffering: "My God, My God, why hast Thou forsaken me?" Her moral loneliness had become a spiritual one, yet, paradoxically, she may well have felt herself at long last within sight of the peaceable kingdom. A puzzle to many of us, ridiculous to many of us: that utter absurdity of faith which Kierkegaard had the intellectual daring to acknowledge, and Simone Weil the existential daring to embody in her life.

Idolatry is due to the fact that, while athirst for absolute good, one is not in possession of supernatural attention, and one has not the patience to let it grow.

Only one thing can be taken as an end, for in relation to the human person it possesses a kind of transcendence: this is the collective. The collective is the object of all idolatry, this it is which chains us to the earth.

Gravity and Grace

7

Idolatry
and the Intellectuals

Among Simone Weil's last essays, "Uprootedness in the Towns"[1] has a singular force and relevance for our times. Weil is at her best as she views the twentieth-century urban scene in France and other Western nations and notes the moral confusion and political dangers – uncertainty, unrest, and a fearful self-interest on everyone's part, because no one is sure what will happen tomorrow. She is particularly concerned with what she calls "the moral well-being of the workman." She looks at the ways factory life influences the ideals and aspirations of those who spend their days in "vast industrial prisons," on the assembly lines in front of dangerous and exhausting machines. She saw, firsthand, the despair among France's 1930s proletariat and tried to imagine a world in which working people would have not only more decent wages and working conditions but also more control and understanding of the lives they lived. Her utopian vision includes not only the dream of a house, "a bit of garden," but also an effort to give workers a sense of how they and their particular work fitted into life's overall scheme – in other words, to restore their roots.

> We must change the system concerning concentration of attention during working hours, the type of stimulants which make for the overcoming of laziness or exhaustion – and which at present are merely fear and extra pay – the type of obedience

135

necessary, the far too small amount of initiative, skill, and thought demanded of workmen, their present exclusion from any imaginative share in the work of the enterprise as a whole, their sometimes total ignorance of the value, social utility, and destination of the things they manufacture, and the complete divorce between working life and family life.

When I hear factory workers[2] talk bluntly about their state of mind, I do not always hear in their statements the self-pity or the discouragement or the sense of worthlessness Simone Weil attributes to those she observed in the Paris of the middle 1930s. I wonder whether they might not find her solutions to their troubles patronizing. Here is a General Motors employee from Framingham, Massachusetts, talking, in 1984.

"Look, it's no picnic, and I know it every day, and say it every day: it's no picnic going to work there [in the factory where he helped make parts for Chevrolet cars]. But I don't go there to have a picnic! I go there to make a living! I don't need anyone feeling sorry for me! They brought in these people, and tried to get us to 'gripe.' I figure: look, I'm not the owner. I haven't got any money. I'm just a guy who works hard and wants a good wage to bring home. Sure, it would be nice if they had better conditions! Sure, it helps to sit and blow off steam – or does it? I don't know! Someone has to do this lousy work, and if it isn't me, it'll be another guy, I guess. I figure: I've got my health, and I'd go nuts without a job, and I bring home a pretty good check, so what the hell! If I had a Sony Walkman playing music in my ears, and a fancy restroom and cafeteria nearby, and some course to take for half an hour at the company's expense – well, I don't know if it'd make one single bit of difference to me, to be honest with you. These people came through here last year, and they gave us questionnaires, and they sat down with us and asked us more and more questions, and I know they were trying to do better by us in the long run, but like I told my daughter afterward: to go to work in that factory will never be to sit and study those Shakespeare plays you're reading for your high school English teacher, and that's that!"

This man's tough pragmatism tells him that there are limits to reform in an enterprise primarily concerned with efficient productivity. And yet that wry reference to Shakespeare reminds one of Simone Weil's hope that France's factory workers would, somehow, live better lives not only materially but morally and spiritually. In this concern Simone Weil was not alone. In the 1920s and 1930s a number of industrial engineers in the United States thought about similar matters and tried – for instance, in the so-called General Electric studies[3] – to ascertain what might make for a livelier, more responsive work force. The motives were not Simone Weil's; they were more economic, but there was a recognition in these studies that workers treated callously will react in certain ways that might result not only in less efficiency but also in a general demoralization of an entire society.

When Simone Weil criticizes advanced industrialism, she reserves a particular criticism for intellectuals. For example, as she tries to describe the consequences of a certain kind of social and economic situation upon human beings, she makes this comparison.

> The majority of workmen have at any rate at this stage of their lives experienced the sensation of no longer existing, accompanied by a sort of inner vertigo, such as intellectuals or bourgeois, even in their greatest sufferings, have very rarely had the opportunity of knowing. This first shock, received at so early an age, often leaves an indelible mark. It can rule out all love of work once and for all.

While the phrase "inner vertigo" is intriguing, how does one establish a scale of suffering and rank people on it? Lots of well-educated people populate our asylums and are disoriented, confused, and by their own descriptions empty or dizzy with doubt. No small number of intellectuals admit to moral and emotional problems, to uncertainty or fearfulness or even paralysis. In the essay "Uprootedness," she goes on to say, "A condition of any working-class culture is the mingling of what are called 'intellectuals' – an awful name, but at present they scarcely deserve a better one – with the workers."[4] Thereby, those intellectuals would somehow become better persons. Writing as if she were outside the class system and able to render judgments in a morally objective manner, she makes a distinction between the people, on the one hand, and intellectuals, the bourgeoisie, the elite, on the other. This is consistent with her scorn for the banality of Marxist rhetoric and Freudian reductionism, her concern for the replacement of one tyranny by another.

When she is writing about literature (novels, poetry, plays) she points out that its "subject . . . is always the human condition." Then she draws this conclusion: "It is the people who have the truest, most direct experience of what this human condition is." She means not all the people, but only certain ones; she uses "the people," in a sociological and political way, as her next sentence makes altogether clear: "On the whole, and saving exceptions, second-class works [of literature] and below are most suitable for the élite, and absolutely first-class works most suitable for the people." In case one still has any doubt, here she is bringing together her beloved Greek literature and her equally beloved working person, a marvelous triumph, arguably, of romantic idealism.

> What an intensity of understanding could spring up from contact between the people and Greek poetry, the almost unique theme of which is misfortune! Only, one would have to know how to translate and present it. A workman, for instance, who bears the anguish of unemployment deep in the very marrow of his bones, would understand the feelings of Philoctetes when his bow is taken away from him, and the despair with which he stares at his powerless hands.

Now, a "bourgeois," she hastens to add, under normal circumstances, would be "absolutely incapable of [such] understanding."

These words,[5] written in her later life, when Simone Weil had every spiritual reason to be less abrasive and scornful, place her squarely in a certain tradition, that of intellectual anti-intellectualism. One thinks immediately of three of her contemporaries, who straddled the worlds she did with the same anxiety and uncertainty and self-accusatory violence. Shortly before she wrote this essay, James Agee, a New York intellectual, would visit Alabama to learn about how America's sharecroppers live; George Orwell would go to Wigan to understand the way England's miners were managing their grim fate; and William Carlos Williams, a doctor to the poor, was climbing up and down the tenement stairs of northern New Jersey's urban slums, and late at night tried to write about those people's struggles, trying to do justice to their language, their feelings, their difficulties, their small moments of triumph, too.

Those three, like Simone Weil, were crossing social and cultural boundaries, trying to put into words what they saw and heard for the benefit of readers who had not visited these foreign lands and for their own benefit as well. As William Carlos Williams once put it, "I know that the people who read me aren't the people who get my writing juices going!" He was thinking of the constant education he received in the homes of New Jersey's Depression-era immigrant poor, their troubles and their fierce determination to prevail, a reminder to him that his own life was not the only kind being lived.

> I am all wrapped up in myself, and my own silly, damn fool worries – and then I'll be going on my rounds, and I'll meet someone who has so much less than I have, who has practically nothing at all, and yet there is so much energy at work, and a lot of savvy, and plenty of guts, and plain, raw, ordinary goodness. I'll feel ashamed of myself – and even sorry for myself. Of course, I wouldn't want to make a switch; I'm staying where I am! It's hard, living with all the thoughts you have on this subject – "them" and you yourself! I try to put the mix of emotions in my work, but I don't always succeed in doing the job right![6]

Williams was well aware of the ironies in this kind of writing.

I'll tell you, vanity is a part of all this, the old Adam: the writer's ego! I get a lot of ideas from my work, but then I'm back in Rutherford, sitting at the typewriter, and my mind goes racing along, and I have to face it, I'm taking the stuff of life, and it's becoming a part of me: their lives get turned into my property! When someone does that, he feels a little funny – maybe ashamed. We know we're lucky, but we know others aren't so lucky; and the unlucky are giving the lucky a big boost. I guess that's the way it is all over – sad for "them," and nice for us! You can get disgusted with the whole scene, though. You can get angry!

Sometimes, Williams pointed out, the ironies and inconsistencies and paradoxes of this life "pile up so high that you're ready to shut up for awhile and let them sink in." On the other hand, he said,

You can go the other way. . . . You can just blow up – find an "enemy" and give it all you've got, with words of anger and frustration! There's nothing like a good target – a place where you can dump all the shame and guilt you feel, all the damn resentments that have been building up in you! . . . When you're all over the map like that, you can turn on yourself hard and mean, call yourself lots of names, or you can find someone you know and do the same with that guy: look at him, the lousy, no-good fool or the moral idiot! Then you walk away, feeling a little better and stronger yourself! It's all our human nature, isn't it? And very sad![7]

Williams's self-accusations as well as the role of the "target" for this thoughtful social observer are reminiscent of Simone Weil. Both can be found in *Let Us Now Praise Famous Men*. James Agee, the Greenwich Village, Harvard-educated writer turns on New York's intellectual world with a vengeance. He also turns on himself as the social essayist on the prowl, poking at a particular rural scene, getting his information, taking off again to turn phrases and mull over his experience. Meanwhile, the tenant families stayed right where they were, in north central Alabama. When the book appeared, they were not celebrated by readers the world over as Agee was destined to be.

James Agee was constantly casting doubt and suspicion on himself, his motives, and his purposes, and he was not loath to turn his considerable fury at others, mocking the pretensions of his fellow writers or of the academic world. At times one wonders what the one (the world of intellectuals) has to do with the other (the world of Southern tenant farmers). Agee, after all, is not trying to do a social and economic study. He is anxious, rather, to do justice to what he called human actuality, and the assaults on intellectuals, it can be maintained, weaken the force and momentum of his argument, distract the reader, and add to the length of a statement already rather extended, even tortured in its manner of presentation. Nevertheless, and despite several years of reflection, of writing and scrapping what was written, he chose to keep in his literary-documentary text passage after passage of anti-intellectual scorn or satire. He can't forget, and won't let us forget, that the very act of reading, as with the act of writing, is a distinct privilege: in Simone Weil's unnerving imagery, a mark of the slave owner, as opposed to the slave.

As for Orwell's *The Road to Wigan Pier*,[8] it so surprised, alarmed, irritated, and troubled the people who commissioned the investigative study in the first place that the publisher, Victor Gollancz, had to write an explanatory foreword, a rebuttal to the second half of the book, which is full of sarcasm directed at England's left-leaning intelligentsia, to which Orwell himself obviously belonged. Like Weil, Williams, and Agee, Orwell hits hard at not only intellectuals, but the "class" to which they, and he, belong, the bourgeoisie. The comforts of a writer can become strange burdens when that writer is describing others who have no such comforts and can never count on obtaining them. Under such circumstances why not lash out loudly at a class of people who have, comparatively, so very much and who also (out of self-knowledge!) will be inclined not only to take such an outburst in stride but even join him or her in self-reproach?

Simone Weil nowhere better reveals her essentially religious confrontation of herself than in her essay "Reflections on the Right Use of School Studies with a View to the Love of God."[9] The title poses, once more, the vexing question of the intellect: What is its correct use and purpose? Amid her suggestions that students and teachers alike take pains to be candid and openhearted with one another and learn from their mistakes, she suddenly offers the following spiritual exhortation:

> Above all it is there that we can acquire the virtue of humility [by taking careful note of our errors, wrong steps as students], and that is a far more precious treasure than all academic progress. From this point of view it is perhaps even more useful to contemplate our stupidity than our sin. Consciousness of sin gives us the feeling that we are evil, and a kind of pride sometimes finds a place in it. When we force ourselves to fix the gaze, not only of our eyes but of our souls, upon a school exercise in which we have failed through sheer stupidity, a sense of our mediocrity is borne in upon us with irresistible evidence. No knowledge is more to be desired. If we can arrive at knowing this truth with all our souls we shall be well established on the right foundation.

There is, obviously, a spiritual link between that declaration and Emerson's[10] telling Harvard students, in his "American Scholar" address, that "character is higher than intellect," or Tolstoy, in his middle years, turning skeptically on his own ambitions and successful talent and following an intense interest in the fate of the poor.[11] My own students, young and aspiring, keep reminding me that these renunciatory gestures have been made by those who have managed to get some good mileage out of their intellects, earned themselves an attentive audience, and are only at that point ready to acknowledge misgivings with respect to intellectual activity. Simone Weil, however, was not a noted, much-published intellectual during her lifetime. Her intellectual celebrity began to occur only years after her death. As noted earlier, what we call her books were, at her death, mostly a series of unpublished letters, essays, and journal entries. True, she was known to certain fellow intellectuals in Paris because of the startling brilliance of the few essays she had published and because she was one of the few writers who had dared work in a factory and had drawn upon such experience in her writing. But in 1943 she was young and obscure.

Her situation was thus different than that of some well-known intellectual who decides to turn critically on his or her own role. Her self-criticism was not the result of a reputation at last secure and solid enough to allow for the ingestion of a measured serving of humble pie. She is quite shrewd in the way she handles her examination of pride, the pride we can take in apologizing for our pride! She contrasts humility with academic progress. Not that she had abandoned her own struggle for academic progress. In her journal entries and letters she remained the erudite reader and writer whose voracious intellectual appetite was ready for any challenge. But one suspects that she was aware of her idiosyncratic nature and might be considered an odd thinker whose ideas don't register with others and is regarded as someone to be tolerated at best.

This loneliness was not for her an occasion of self-pity. She really did want to exert her influence on others, most especially on her country's ongoing political and military history. She knew that she was bright, had a sharp and original mind, and could put down her thoughts in strong, arresting prose. But she also knew that something in her was inadequate to the influence she yearned to exert. This felt inadequacy may have given her honest access to the humility she sought. It was not false modesty that led her to write, in a July 1943 letter to her parents[12] a month before she died:

> Some people feel in a confused way that there is something to what she has been saying, arguing for. But once they have made a few polite remarks about my intelligence their conscience is

clear. After which, they listen to me or read me with the same hurried attention which they give to everything, making up their minds definitely about each separate little hint of an idea as soon as it appears: "I agree with this," "I don't agree with that," "This is marvelous," "That is completely idiotic" (the latter antithesis comes from my chief). In the end they say: "Very interesting," and pass on to something else. They have avoided fatigue. What else can one expect? I am convinced that the most fervent Christians among them don't concentrate their attention much more when they are praying or reading the Gospel. Why imagine it is better elsewhere? I have seen some of those elsewheres. As for posterity, before there is a generation with muscle and power of thought the books and manuscripts of our day will surely have disappeared.

I have always found that particular letter especially touching. So much of her attitude toward herself comes across, gently, without the stridency she sometimes displays. It is the letter of a committed intellectual. It is the letter of a person who wants a serious, thoughtful audience, people who share her concerns and are willing to pay attention. It is also the letter of someone well aware of her own failure to reach and affect others, and their resulting indifference to her mind's efforts. It is the letter of a woman who, though still in her early thirties, has an exceptional sense of history – the ability to look beyond the confines of her life, her era, her century, or more. While she shows every intention of keeping her own considerable muscle and power mobilized, at the service of the French cause, she has found a quiet resignation. Perhaps she sensed that death was not far away. Intellectuals rarely find that kind of resignation within themselves, even when they are a half century older than she was, and even when all their writing has been published and well received.

At other times her writing showed her anxious, troubled, afraid of going through life ignored or rebuked. On such occasions her verbal thrusts at intellectuals are not unlike those of Flannery O'Connor, who was much interested in and appreciative of Weil's essays.[13] They were both loners, both exceptionally talented, both with an uneasy relationship to the intellectual circles of their time. In contrast, Simone de Beauvoir, who was a fellow student of Weil's at the Sorbonne, had a relaxed enjoyment of intellectual life that was never available to Weil.

Just as O'Connor fires away sarcastically at "interleckchuals," at Manhattan and all its sophistication and literary power, Simone Weil kept her distance from literary salons in Paris, even turning on such Catholic intellectuals as Jacques Maritain. Her moral and emotional affinity was with Georges Bernanos.[14] They both were outsiders, spiritually solitary, ardently French, profoundly affected by the life of Jesus and the humble, poor, deeply compassionate life he led. Both drew a personal lesson from that life. Even as Jesus did not sit around discussing ideas with learned ones, they tried hard to keep their own company and to celebrate the obscure goodness of those who are silent and impoverished.

No matter the intensity of her religious contemplation, Simone Weil was always watchful for the intrusions of the intellect. In her New York notebooks she remarks on those who can be found "reducing the bread and wine of the Eucharist to a mere symbol."[15] She is aware how tempting such an interpretation is for so-called Christian intellectuals. But she will have no part of all that: "The mysteries then cease to be an object of contemplation; they are no longer of any use. This is a case of the illegitimate use of the intelligence, and one may think that the soul of those who entertain these speculations has not yet been illumined by supernatural love." Flannery O'Connor once insisted, in her equally uncompromising way, that "the task of the novelist is to deepen mystery, and mystery is a great embarrassment to the modern mind."[16]

Again and again Simone Weil characterizes that "modern mind" as not only egoistic, but idolatrous, taken with its own prowess and accomplishments. Like Flannery O'Connor, once more, she was aware of idolatry as a constant danger to us all, though she concluded that some centuries and cultures were more the victims (and perpetrators) of that idolatry than others. Even as a young schoolteacher she was trenchant as well as charming in her analysis of intellectual authority – the manner in which we elevate a body of knowledge and those who have contributed to it or teach it. She saw such elevation as a dangerous ritual. She was quick to spot "pitiless bureaucrats" who perpetuated such rituals, whether in universities and schools or in the factories where she worked. In a lovely and openhearted letter to a pupil[17] ("My dear child"), she tells of her struggle, at the age of twenty-six, to break away from such a mode of thinking. "Above all, I feel I have escaped from a world of abstractions, to find myself among real men – some good and some bad, but with a real goodness or badness."

Throughout her intellectual life, she realized that a danger of that life is a particular kind of idolatry, whereby the person who lives by ideas ends up treating them with an excessive reverence. In that same letter to a student she refers to egoism as something "which revolts me." But she is not being moralistic at this point as she would be, at times, in the near future, but rather, the psychologist. She grants that egoism "clearly does not prevent love." Egotists embrace each other, fall in love, live in apparent contentment. The problem, she has begun to realize, is not the presence in our lives of egoism, but whether it leads us to live "among phantoms, dreaming instead of living." The phantoms she mentions are constructions of the mind, of its "unreflecting egoism" (again, George Eliot's phrase) at work. "Egoism leads one to consider the people one loves as mere occasions of joy or suffering and to forget completely that they exist in their own right." She has in her own searching, yet almost casual way, in a letter to a schoolchild, put her finger on a central psychological maneuver at work in idolatry – the absorption of the world's reality into one's own, after which, what we see of the world and respond to in it is, in reality, ourselves disguised.

A few years later, in New York, she carried this insight further. "Thoughts are fluid, they are swayed by fantasy, passion, fatigue. But work has to be carried on persistently, for many hours a day, every day. Therefore motives are required which are proof against the instability of thoughts, that is to say, against *relation*; in other words, what is required is absolutes, or idols."[18] She regards us as going through constant ups and downs in our thinking and feeling life, hence craving some fixed star, some rudder to help us steer, give us a sense that we are in control. In a memorably terse judgment, she concludes, "Therefore, in the Cave the idolatrous passions are a necessity." She then becomes the resigned policy analyst: "What is needed is to find the least bad idols."

She would never, however, really be satisfied with what is "least bad." She wanted more for her schoolchildren, her fellow factory workers or field hands, and for the people of her beloved France. She wanted its citizens to be freed of the peculiar idolatry that nationalism generates, especially in the modern, secular mind: the nation-state as an ultimate reality. It was her early genius, after all, which recognized the "great beast" – militarism and chauvinism – as terribly dangerous and demoralizing. Even the Greeks, whom she cherished so dearly, fell prey to that kind of idolatry. Moreover, she had spotted idolatry in the Soviet Union early on, tracing its history: Marx's acquiescence, which took place long before Lenin was buried in a mausoleum and Stalin became the god of the Russians. When a scholar averts his eyes to the serious difficulties his own analytic thinking has produced, he is neglecting what *is* in favor of what he is trying to create.

In her own way, Simone Weil was attempting to construct a theory of moral psychology, not psychopathology. She watched carefully for lapses in logic. "To regard the *normal* as a *particular case* of the abnormal (and the conscious as a particular case of the unconscious) is the same sort of inversion as to regard arithmetical numbers as a particular case of complex numbers, or mechanical energy as a particular case of electrical energy. Already in Leibniz: the equal as a particular case of the unequal."[19] This observation did not mean that she denied the usefulness of many of Freud's propositions. Elsewhere in her notebooks she had concluded that "Freud is right" insofar as he had claimed that "every attachment is of the same nature as sexuality."[20] This very allegation on the part of Freud was the one that made him so frightening, so outrageous to others. Though prudish, she did not flee the new knowledge of psychoanalysis. She took aim, rather, at the hunger of the psychoanalytic theorist who won't settle for the empirically grounded studies in sexuality, but who wants to go much further, to base universal laws on these suggestive findings. To this day the problem of logic that she dared question persists as a "problem in theory" in the profession: the relationship between the abnormal and the normal.

Simone Weil was also aware of the irony of Freud's calling religion an illusion – he who handed rings to those in his circle, as he called it, and he whose picture would itself become a revered object in so many offices. The sectarian splits and schisms in this twentieth-century mode of inquiry which was so proudly and emphatically declared an aspect of science by the "founding father" in his book *The Future of an Illusion*, among other texts, would not have surprised her. Even the most conventional of sciences, the hardest of the hard, she pointed out, lent themselves to idolatry. "Scientists believe in science in the same way that the majority of Catholics believe in the Church, namely as Truth crystallized in an infallible collective opinion; they contrive to believe this in spite of the continual changes in theory. In both cases it is through lack of faith in God."

Could she possibly have isolated herself further – in one fell swoop taking on the two major sources of this century's "faith"? She pursues the matter forcefully, unashamedly. "A Catholic directs his thought secondarily towards the truth, but primarily towards conformity with the Church's doctrine." Then she adds, "A scientist does the same, only in this case there is no established doctrine but a collective opinion in process of formation." That collective opinion can be not only helpful and instructive to those anxious to learn more, but also an instrument of control, a means by which compliance is exacted and disagreement punished.

Finally, as she saw it, there are only two alternatives.

One has only the choice between God and idolatry. There is no other possibility. For the faculty of worship is in us, and it is either directed somewhere into this world, or into another. If one affirms God one is either worshipping God or else some things of this world labelled with his name. If one denies God, either one is worshipping him unknown to oneself or else one is worshipping some things of this world in the belief that one sees them only as such, but in fact, though unknown to oneself, imagining the attributes of Divinity in them.

Idolatry is in our very nature, she is declaring, and when disguised (as scientific pursuit, as politics, as a deep affection for nature, as a religious ritual and practice) is no less what it is, though perhaps more dangerous, potentially, because not even acknowledged. If only some of us who have been psychoanalyzed, and who look deeply into the psychological life of others, were able to be so forcefully analytic about ourselves! I remember an aphorism I used to hear from William Carlos Williams as he went from home to home, making his rounds, still recovering, he'd say, from some disappointment or serious impasse in his "other life," that of the writer. "It's gold or glory or God – what people worship." Once when I added the worship intellectuals accord their own ideas and theories, he replied curtly, annoyed with my lack of imagination, "I think that comes under glory, or maybe God!"

Simone Weil's concern with idolatry was directed inward as well as toward the two "religions" of her time. Simone Weil was trying hard to sort out her own beliefs, and as an intellectual, she realized, that continuing effort "marked" her. She kept describing herself as enslaved. There is at work in her prolonged analysis of idolatry a compelling self-scrutiny worthy of those Christian saints she admired, and too, of the young Freud taking a bold, unflinching look inward, no matter how uncomfortable the effort.

"No human being escapes the necessity of conceiving some good outside himself toward which his thought turns in a movement of desire, supplication, and hope," she wrote in her notebook while she was in New York City.[21] She continues in this vein, yet again connecting a general psychological statement – idolatry as a major mode of expression for everyone – to her personal search. "Consequently, the only choice is between worshipping the true God or an idol. Every atheist is an idolater – unless he is worshipping the true God in his impersonal aspect. The majority of the pious are idolaters."

She distinguished between faith and belief; the latter, she said, can be an anxious or self-serving act of ingratiation with respect to an institution: the Church. No matter her often stated love for the Catholic Church, there was something quite stubbornly Protestant in her wish to stand alone before God, to wait for grace on her very own. She struck hard at any institution, including the Catholic Church, which she may have felt stood in her way.

Again one has to remember the time in which Simone Weil was writing these words about the Catholic Church in the notebooks she kept in New York. In the dark days of the Second World War (1942), she saw little indication that the Catholic Church in the United States (or France, not to mention Germany and Italy) had any great interest in standing up to what surely was an anti-Christ to match any other the world had ever seen. Her position was a difficult one; she was drawn strongly – passionately may be the correct word – to an institution she knew to be severely flawed. She could not content herself, however, with the knowledge that all institutions are flawed, even as all human beings are utterly imperfect. She was a perfectionist in religious matters, too. Just as she was prepared to sacrifice herself to be rid of her imperfections, she was not inclined to be tolerant of the sins of omission on the part of "principalities and powers."

Yet even in this time of personal and historical turmoil, she could mobilize within herself the penetrating lucidity and logic for which she is known. She sees a way to come to terms with idolatry. "A power comes to reside in any object which has been approached with intense feeling by large numbers of men. To adore this power is idolatry. True adoration consists in contemplating such an object with the thought that it has become divine through a convention ratified by God."

The first sentence of that observation would not offend most reasonable people. The second would be more controversial. The word *adore* is crucial – if "intense feeling" has turned to "adoration," a significant psychological shift has taken place, one which may well not be fully recognized. How many of us in psychoanalytic psychiatry, for example, are willing to regard our intense feeling with respect to Freud's writing – indeed all his words, even his casual or off-the-cuff remarks – as a matter of adoration? Perhaps we repress more than our sexual and aggressive drives; perhaps we can't recognize the strong urge we have to become adoring.

The third sentence in that assertion was, of course, the decisive one for Simone Weil; it is with that escalation of her thought, into the realm of religious faith, that she would lose the assent, maybe even the interest, of many intellectuals who otherwise found her writing provocative, if not congenial. Yet this statement is central to her thought. In the last years of her life she worried that all beliefs, even religious ones, risk idolatry. Her insistence upon "a convention ratified by God" is another example of the thoroughly personal knowledge of God that she sought, and one gathers, believed herself to have obtained. She seems persuaded that under the auspices of the Church such personal knowledge simply does not come about; on the contrary, parishioners turn idolatrous and mistake a ritual, a habit, and alas, a social custom (to go to church on Sunday, say) for such a convention.

She had quite obviously been yearning for even more than such a contemplation of divinity; she craved an ultimate or transcendent conversation with God. This kind of faith – an existentialism of a rather special and demanding kind – puts her in the company of Kierkegaard rather than Pascal:[22] a Protestant rather than Catholic existentialism. True, many of the Catholic Church's saints have sought and claimed those "conversations," but have done so under the sanction of the Church. Their experience of God has been far less lonely or even anti-institutional than the kind Simone Weil probably had in mind, or experienced at one time or another.

Toward the end of her life, this struggle with idolatry was never far from her thoughts. Simone Weil was always on the scent, it seems, for those who did not know their own intense feelings, their own inclination to adore. It may well be that she was engaged in a fight to the death, literally, with her own idolatrous inclinations. She knew the twentieth-century temptations of the "intellectual flesh." She knew how seductive Marxist thought had been to those with a passion for more social and political and economic equity in this world. She knew how seductive science had been to those who were anxious to have a direct, tangible influence on the world, on matter, on the way we live our lives. She knew how seductive psychology and psychoanalysis had been for intellectuals who were eager to understand not only matter but mind.

All of us who have lived in this century can remember this idée fixe or that one, the torrent of passion which various discoveries, breakthroughs, and new paradigms have prompted. My father was an engineer; he knew the slogan "Better living through chemistry"; he knew what "the great engineer" had promised America – the line of hope and trust and unbridled expectation that went from Alexander Graham Bell to Thomas Edison to Henry Ford to the Massachusetts Institute of Technology, where he studied, to radar, atoms penetrated and smashed, antibiotics, genes unlocked, computers, and lasers. He was alive, as I wrote these words; he was born under Queen Victoria, in Yorkshire, England, and lived through eighty-five years of this century, long enough to know what nuclear physics and the rest of science could end up doing to all of us. He had watched, as he once told me, "a parade of promises arrive," only to disappoint, one after the other. Though he was sure that this life will become more secure, will turn into a more inviting and promising one for more and more people, in his ninth decade he knew a doubt, an uncertainty, that he would once have found foreign. And so, I notice, it goes with a good number of my students, sixty and more years his junior. They, too, are grateful for the obvious "progress" of these past decades, yet they also shudder in the face of this century's death camps and its technology of murder and of war.

For them, Simone Weil is no stranger. Hers was a modern pilgrimage; she entertained all our assumptions, presumptions, and anticipations – her journey is ours. She experienced, in the few years she knew among us, our buoyancy, our optimism, and soon enough, our terrible discouragement and melancholy. She saw Pandora's box open, revealing its cheap tricks, its deceptions. She saw clear skies cloud up overnight. She saw all the castles we have built in those skies; she entered them, took their measure, and left with tears or anger, bitterness. In the end only one sight was left for her eyes; in the end, that modern pilgrimage so swiftly concluded, she looked upward, affirmed unflinchingly her last hope, the hope of heaven – and died, one suspects, glad at last, glad to be hurrying home, to be with God, with history's, time's incarnation of him, Jesus, and with her mind's incarnation of him, Plato; and, she must have fervently expected, with more "conversations" ahead.

Notes

Preface

1. I have described some of those conversations in *Children of Crisis: A Study of Courage and Fear* (Boston: Atlantic/Little, Brown, 1967).

2. See "The Meaning of Work," *Atlantic Monthly* (October 1971); "A Prophet of Grace," *The American Scholar* (Autumn 1973); "Simone Weil," *The Washington Post*, December 26, 1976; "Simone Weil's Mind," in *Simone Weil: Interpretations of a Life*, ed. George Abbott White (Amherst: University of Massachusetts Press, 1981); "Gravity and Grace in the Novel *A Confederacy of Dunces*," a lecture published by the University of Southwestern Louisiana, Lafayette, 1981; "Simone Weil's Faith," *New Oxford Review* (September 1982); and Eric Springsted, Introduction to *Simone Weil and the Suffering of Love* (Cambridge, Mass.: Cowley Press, 1986).

3. The editor, Kai Erikson, was most helpful in prompting me to reassess Simone Weil's ideas, her writing, and her manner of regarding the world. See "Simone Weil: The Mystery of Her Life," *Yale Review* (Winter 1984).

4. The conference was held at the Massachusetts Institute of Technology in the fall of 1975.

5. I could not have attempted this book without Miss Freud's constant clarifications and encouragement and without, too, her willingness to throw her hands up in the air, at certain points, with an admission of frank ignorance or perplexity.

Chapter 1
Introduction to a Life

1. Simone Weil was frank to say, on another occasion, that she herself was not all that "hopeful" at times – that indeed, she was quite "worried," and even "gloomy about our [England's] prospects."

2. Simone Weil's biographer Simone Pétrement mentions those worries, and her brother remembers them.

3. James Agee's *Let Us Now Praise Famous Men* (Boston: Houghton Mifflin, 1960) offers one of the best discussions of this complex matter – the lessons to be learned by a "privileged" outsider among the poor. In the companion volume to this one, on Dorothy Day, *Dorothy Day: A Radical Devotion* (Reading, Mass.: Addison-Wesley, 1987), this question comes up repeatedly – a constant struggle for her.

4. Again, there was a personal emphasis, I thought, to those words as they were spoken.

5. His poems were companions of sorts to her, not unlike their role in Dorothy Day's life.

6. Still, it was an extremely serious, life-threatening disease, a fact understandably hard for us to realize today.

7. The contrast between this letter and her writing while she was in exile in New York tells us a great deal about Simone Weil and gives us a measure of her mental and spiritual situation at the end of her life.

Chapter 2
Her Hunger

1. Simone Weil may well have meant these words literally. Her passion for France was an important part of her life, strengthened,

of course, by the war and its tragic consequences. Even as Orwell
had at that time become rather emotionally nationalistic (for example, in *The English People*, about the character of its citizenry),
Simone Weil had by then abandoned her critical attitude with
respect to politics, her inclination to be skeptical of anything and
anyone, in favor of a passionate embrace of *la patrie*. For her this
was the nation of Racine and Pascal, and in her dreams, the nation
which would in the future offer the world an embodiment of the
Platonic ideals she cherished.

2. He had treated many such patients. I remember accompany-
ing him on his visits to them, and his admonition, "Keep eating!"

3. We don't know what facts reached her, never mind the feelings which affected her perception of them.

4. Her determination, her resolve, is apparent; its sources, again,
elude us.

5. A brave claim, unlikely to prove true. What is of interest
here is her grant of autonomy to the mind – its serene independence
from the travail of the body.

6. See David B. Herzog and Paul M. Copeland, "Eating Disor-
ders," *New England Journal of Medicine*, August 1, 1985;
"Anorexia Nervosa" in Gill's *Textbook of Medicine* (Philadelphia:
Saunders, 1979).

7. I have discussed these final moments in the essay "Simone
Weil: The Mystery of Her Life" (see note 3, Preface).

8. I urge the interested reader to consult Rudolph M. Bell, *Holy
Anorexia* (Chicago: University of Chicago Press, 1985). This book
explains in great detail the long tradition in Christianity of fierce
abstinence from food.

9. If her struggle with her pride is obvious, the dramatic, if not
hysterical nature of that struggle is no less obvious. Did Weil ever
wonder what the God to whom she prayed thought of such decla-
rations, this God who fed and healed and comforted so many
Galileans almost two thousand years ago? She seemed to have
little interest in Jesus as a healer. An important contrasting view
is presented by Stanley Hauerwas in *Suffering Presence* (Notre
Dame, Ind.: University of Notre Dame Press, 1986), an eloquent,

tightly argued case for healing as a moral act. He speaks of suffering as a challenge to our compassion rather than as evidence of a Christian testimony or a badge of merit.

10. Had she lived, she might well have found Barth the most congenial of theologians: his stern orthodoxy appealing and his conservatism, in part, akin to hers. On the other hand, she had a radical, egalitarian side which would have prompted her to confront Barth, and one suspects, some of her more traditional or conservative admirers. See, for instance, Karl Barth, *Evangelical Theology* (New York: Holt, Rinehart and Winston, 1963).

11. Georges Bernanos delivers a similar message at the end of *Diary of a Country Priest*, when he has the dying priest say, "How easy it is to hate oneself! True grace is to forget. Yet if pride could die in us, the supreme grace would be to love oneself in all simplicity – as one would love any of those who themselves have suffered and loved in Christ."

12. Helen Ross, a psychoanalyst and a good friend of Anna Freud's, suggested to me years ago that I read Knut Hamsun, *Hunger*, with an introduction by Isaac Bashevis Singer, trans. Robert Bly (New York: Farrar, Straus and Giroux, 1967), as a means of thinking about Simone Weil. I subsequently wrote an essay on the novel, "Knut Hamsun's Morning and Evening," *New Republic*, September 23, 1967, and found it as helpful as Miss Ross suggested it might be. She died many years ago, but I still remember with gratitude several helpful conversations with her in which Simone Weil's personality figured, and I remember Miss Ross's characterization during one of them: "Such a vexing, turbulent one – it's a wonder she rescued her gifts from the jaws of her demons!"

13. See Hamsun, *Hunger*.

14. In this regard, conversations with Gordon Harper, a psychoanalyst at the Harvard Medical School and the Children's Hospital in Boston have been particularly helpful.

Chapter 3
Her Jewishness

1. Students who read this letter invariably come talk to me about it, wondering what in the world prompted it, and invariably propose self-hatred as the answer – to the point that when one of them comes to see me after class with a frown or a look of anger on his or her face, I know what to expect.

2. I strongly recommend, for contextual reading, Michael R. Marrus and Robert O. Paxton, *Vichy France and the Jews* (New York: Basic Books, 1981). This book offers a terrible indictment not only of Vichy France, but the entire West (including the United States), for indifference to what was happening then to Europe's Jews. It makes clear that even the Vatican was not about to challenge the Vichy anti-Semitic statutes.

3. This letter, too, saddens or enrages many of my students, Jewish and non-Jewish alike.

4. Nor do we know precisely which of those reports she read and which were assigned to her for comment, as against those which caught her interest.

5. See, again, *Vichy France and the Jews*, in which Simone Weil's letter, and the position she sets forth in it, is mentioned.

6. These opinions are another source of great provocation for readers who become interested enough in Simone Weil's life to encounter them.

7. Needless to say, the phrase "protective measures" has also appalled readers, not to mention this writer.

8. Ronald Steel, *Walter Lippmann and the American Century* (Boston: Atlantic Monthly Press, 1980).

9. She hands down this judgment *ex cathedra*, with no effort to argue or convince.

10. In her notion that intellectuals have a lot to learn by leaving urban, metropolitan centers in favor of the countryside, Weil anticipated Mao Tse-tung by a generation or more.

11. See Martin Buber, *Good and Evil* (New York: Scribner's, 1953), and Martin Buber, *I and Thou*, trans. Walter Kaufmann

(New York: Scribner's, 1970). See also Gershom Scholem, *The Messianic Idea in Judaism, and Other Essays in Jewish Spirituality* (New York: Schocken, 1974).

12. These notes or asides were the work of a mind at residence in a body that was fragile and pain-racked by migraine and developing tuberculosis. Had Weil lived they might have been discarded in private as the foolish speculation to which we are all privy, and which few share with the world. Again, it is important to remember that she never chose to publish the vast majority of what she wrote as entries in her journals or notebooks. Thomas Merton, in a note on Simone Weil (vol. 17 in his collected papers, on file at Gethsemane, Kentucky) describes some of these as "disorganized material." Merton was obviously touched by her fiery spirit and by her rebelliousness and its counterpart, a wish to be tamed. (Only God could tame her, as she made clear.)

13. As in the previous footnote, one wonders what she might have done with such a remark, particularly had she been pressed by historians for her evidence.

14. Spoken in the course of a personal interview, January 10, 1963, in Atlanta, Georgia.

Chapter 4
Her Political Life

1. In his poem "September 1, 1939."

2. Her friend Simone Pétrement describes their encounter in her biography.

3. There was another side of Bernanos, too, the royalist who belonged to the reactionary, anti-Semitic *Action Française*, founded by Charles Maurras, with whom he broke decisively in the 1930s, when his social and political thinking gradually changed. Like Weil, he worked with the de Gaulle Resistance; indeed, he was one of de Gaulle's strongest advocates until a postwar disillusionment set in: the "factionalization of the parties" which prompted him, yet again, to go into exile, this time to Tunisia, where he died in 1948.

4. In the same spirit, actually, that of disenchantment with a political cause.

5. Orwell, too, lost a few illusions in the encounter with Stalin's long arm at work in Spain.

6. Christopher Lasch, *The Culture of Narcissism* (New York: W. W. Norton, 1979), offers one of the best descriptions of this development and the most thoughtful analysis of what it means.

7. A part of the long essay "Reflections Concerning the Causes of Liberty and Social Oppression."

8. It is remarks such as this one which reveal the raw assertiveness of her mind and its capacity to give itself all too much authority — to be heedless of what obtains every day in the world. For such a mind decreation was a formidable task, indeed.

9. She does not discuss an association of journalists, an editorial board, whereby collective decisions are made and votes taken — not an unknown practice in journalism.

10. An irony not always noted by some who find his writings of interest. I struggle with Rousseau, with that irony, among others, in *Irony in the Mind's Life* (Charlottesville: University of Virginia Press, 1974).

11. In this connection, I have tried to discuss the struggles both these writers waged: *Agee* (New York: Holt, Rinehart and Winston, 1985) and "George Orwell's Sensibility" in *Reflections on America*, ed. Robert Mulvihill (Athens: University of Georgia Press, 1986).

12. This side of her was appealing to Dorothy Day, who read and often commented on certain passages from *The Need for Roots*.

Chapter 5
Her Moral Loneliness

1. Camus was devoted to Simone Weil and to her memory. On the day he was notified that he had received the Nobel Prize, he paid a visit to her mother's postwar Paris home.

2. This social comment was understandably stimulated by the totalitarianism she was witnessing and is, perhaps, somewhat

rhetorical. After all, she was thinking, and the 1930s prompted a wide-ranging literary and philosophical body of thought.

3. She possessed a capacity for scorn, for satire, and for ironic detachment similar to Kierkegaard's.

4. Lasch and Simone Weil share an originality and boldness of social and political analysis: an ability and willingness to draw upon, when necessary, so-called conservative or liberal or reformist or radical thinking, to develop their own way of seeing things.

5. See, again, my analytic struggle and personal response to this book in *Agee* (New York: Holt, Rinehart and Winston, 1985).

6. T. S. Eliot's enthusiasm for this aspect of her writing has been influential in bringing her to the attention of many readers who might otherwise not have encountered her.

7. Here she is at her bravest, daring to part company with many of her intellectual friends and, one suspects, delighted to do so.

8. For this reader a disappointingly mean-spirited response. Dorothy Day's appraisal: "Pure-nonsense. We need to pray for each other all the time, of course, and especially so for her at such a moment, in connection with such a comment (personal interview, February 1972).

Chapter 6
A Radical Grace

1. One of the most widely read pieces Simone Weil wrote, though it was not meant for anyone save Father Perrin. Her parents might have had their own ideas as to whether she was "born" and "grew up" in what she calls the Christian inspiration.

2. Simone Weil and Pascal, however, did have much in common: both were comfortable in the arts and the sciences; both lived relatively brief, brilliant lives; neither married; each was drawn to religion, to the Catholic faith, and both are known to us primarily through their literary and moral legacy.

3. Though, as I point out, it is easy to emphasize the psychiatric side of migraine, we often forget genetics and biology – the physiology of a particular brain, the location of its blood vessels, its neuro-

chemistry. What do we say about those who are full of rage, who acknowledge that they are, but who *don't* ever get migraine headaches? The issue is not only emotional, but the particularity of response in one or another person's body *and* what that response then gets going in the mind. I refer the reader to an excellent essay, "Disease as a Reflection of the Psyche," by Marcia Angell in *New England Journal of Medicine*, June 13, 1985.

4. The title patly describes her attitude – her eagerness for God to find her, rather than for her to go forth and embrace Him, as do those who seek baptism.

5. One thinks, though, of Dorothy Day's humility and of Peter Maurin's, no matter their membership in a Church they believed to be Christ's chosen one.

6. A wonderfully knowing description of what we today call narcissism, including its unconscious aspects.

7. She identified particularly with the pastoral side of Jesus' ministry – the concern for the poor, the embrace of the ostracized, the powerless.

8. One worries, at certain moments in her New York notebooks, whether a desperation of mind has not prompted a perverse idiosyncrasy of analysis. At times her entries are murky and unintelligible, at least to this reader.

9. How that statue engages with the moral and spiritual lives of various *favelados*! The interested reader might want to consult two books of mine in which some of those people of Rio de Janeiro speak, *The Moral Life of Children* and *The Political Life of Children* (Boston: Atlantic Monthly Press, 1986).

10. Nothing in my profession of psychoanalytic psychiatry quite prepared me to comprehend such devastating words – their mix of coherence and overwhelming self-arraignment. The prayer can be found in *First and Last Notebooks* (London: Oxford University Press, 1970).

11. As with the anorexia described in *Holy Anorexia* (see note 8, Chapter 2).

12. Dorothy Day once made the same connection when we spoke about Saint Thérèse (February 1972).

Chapter 7
Idolatry and the Intellectuals

1. The first of three essays on uprootedness in *The Need for Roots*, the other two dealing with uprootedness in the countryside and uprootedness and nationhood. The essay is in many respects a model of social analysis, a marvelous mix of cultural, historical, and psychological observations in a tightly argued presentation.

2. Among them men and women who also work in a General Motors plant in Framingham, Massachusetts. See also *The Middle Americans* (Boston: Atlantic/Little, Brown, 1971), in which the interviews with factory workers reveal their lack of interest either in pity or patronization, and "Workers Who Write about Factory Life Can Be Riveting," *Wall Street Journal*, January 14, 1986.

3. The studies were conducted by F. J. Roethlisberger and W. J. Dickson and published as *Management and the Worker* (Cambridge: Harvard University Press, 1939).

4. One of a number of negative asides directed at "intellectuals"; the quotation marks are a reflection of her attitude.

5. Again from the essay "Uprootedness in the Towns."

6. Remarks made in the course of an afternoon meeting, June 1956. I discuss this aspect of Williams's writing in *William Carlos Williams: The Knack of Survival in America* (New Brunswick, N.J.: Rutgers University Press, 1975, 1983).

7. Similar reflections have been gathered together, with an essay by Dr. Williams's physician son, William Eric Williams, and an introduction by me, under the title *The Doctor Stories* (New York: New Directions, 1984).

8. It is, really, two books, the first part a documentary story of coal miners whom Orwell met in 1936 in Lancashire, the second a vigorous polemic directed at England's socialist intelligentsia.

9. A part of the book published posthumously as *Waiting for God*.

10. An interesting new series of reflections on Emerson, on his struggles with moral and political matters, is Irving Howe, *The American Newness* (Cambridge: Harvard University Press, 1986).

Howe doesn't mention Simone Weil, but he does connect – or rather contrast – the Emersonian emphasis on the self with Ignazio Silone's twentieth-century vision of a common solidarity, a vision not unlike that of Weil as she formulated it in the essays that make up *The Need for Roots*.

11. As in "Confession" or in the novel *Resurrection* or the essays such as "The Kingdom of God Is Within You."

12. The self-dramatizing side of Weil comes across in this letter – her consciousness of the impression she made on others.

13. Flannery O'Connor put *her* sense of the dramatic (see above footnote) into her stories. Needless to say, they shared a fervent Catholic sensibility.

14. Apart from the letters she addressed to him, she mentions him in *The Need for Roots*. She paid him close, admiring heed.

15. She anticipated the wariness, in our own time, of psychological reductionism.

16. A wonderful phrase to be found in Flannery O'Connor's *Mystery and Manners* (New York: Farrar, Straus and Giroux, 1961).

17. Dorothy Day once told me how much she loved that letter (August 1972).

18. These reflections were the basis for a book on political psychology and twentieth-century European social history that she never wrote.

19. Anna Freud was much taken with this statement, which might have been posted on the first page of her *Normality and Pathology in Childhood* (New York: International Universities Press, 1965).

20. Without being too grateful to him, though. Simone Weil seems to regard him, at best, as a gifted essayist who is sometimes on target, sometimes way off the mark.

21. As she wrote this she was slipping rapidly downhill in mind and body. Her struggles with life itself – her complex spiritual life, her turbulent psychological life – are all too evident in these journal entries.

22. Still, her personal and intellectual affinities to Pascal, as mentioned earlier, are striking to contemplate, and Pascal, it can be argued, had his own "Protestant" side: his philosophical affirmations convey a loneliness, an ironic posture with regard to man's religious life, which strike one as far from the Catholic spirit of his era or, indeed, of any era.

Selected Bibliography

The most important of Simone Weil's voluminous essays, letters, and journal excerpts have been collected and published as books. It is important to remember, however, that Simone Weil never sent a manuscript to a book publisher, and for all we know, never intended to do so. Nor did she publish a lot of articles or reviews in magazines, quarterlies, and newspapers. She was a prolific writer, but most of what she wrote during her lifetime was never sent anywhere – it was kept in notebooks, sent as letters to friends, or handed to others, to be held safely for some future day. The last three years of her life were far from settled. She moved from Paris to Marseille to New York and then to London, while Europe was consumed by war. Her health was declining. Not only had she little expectation, it seems, of surviving the war, she may also have wondered, in those dark days, if Western civilization would survive, either. Still, to the end, she jotted notes to herself and wrote to those she loved or respected. What are now called her books are assemblages of her writing, given a title, and arranged by editors with a view to topical or thematic consistency.

In French the titles are *La Pesanteur et la grâce* (Plon, 1948), *La condition ouvrière* (Gallimard, 1951), *L'enracinement* (Gallimard, 1949). Gallimard has also published *Écrits historiques et politiques* (1960), her uncompleted play, *Venise Sauvée*, her *Pensées sous ordre concernant l'amour de Dieu* (1962), and such religious writing as *La Connaissance Surnaturelle* (1950), *Lettre à un religieux* (1951), *Attente de Dieu* (1950), and *Intuitions Pré-Chrétiennes* (1951).

For those who speak English, her writing has been well translated and repeatedly published in England and the United States. I mentioned in the Preface the three major books published early in the 1950s by G. P. Putnam's; they have since gone into a number of paperback editions. The authors of the prefaces to the three volumes are well worth mentioning: T. S. Eliot (*The Need for Roots*); Leslie Fiedler (*Waiting for God*); and Gustave Thibon (*Gravity and Grace*). Each of these writers responds to Simone Weil differently, of course, but the extraordinary depth of feeling and the intensity of respect they show her are in themselves an important testimony to what she has come to mean the world over, for so large a number of men and women.

Other collections of her writing include *On Science, Necessity and the Love of God*, essays edited by Richard Rees (New York: Oxford University Press, 1968); *Simone Weil: Seventy Letters*, also translated by Richard Rees (New York: Oxford University Press, 1965), and by the same editor and publisher, *Simone Weil: First and Last Notebooks* (1970), as well as *Simone Weil: Selected Essays* (1962); *Simone Weil: Oppression and Liberty*, introduced by F. C. Elbert (Amherst: University of Massachusetts Press, 1973); *Simone Weil: Formative Writings, 1929–1941*, ed. Dorothy Tuck McFarland and Wilhelmina van Ness (Amherst: University of Massachusetts Press, 1987); *Intimations of Christianity Among the Ancient Greeks*, ed. Elisabeth Chase Geissbuhler (London: Routledge and Kegan Paul, 1957); *The Notebooks of Simone Weil*, 2 vol., trans. Arthur Wills (London: Routledge and Kegan Paul, 1956). There is, too, *The Simone Weil Reader*, ed. George A. Panichas (New York: David McKay, 1977; paperback, Mount Kisco, N.Y.: Moyer Bell, 1985).

To move from the primary sources to a body of exegesis, comment, criticism, and biographical inquiry, the most ambitious effort is that of Simone Pétrement, a lifelong friend of Simone Weil's – *Simone Weil: A Life* (New York: Pantheon, 1976). Other helpful books are *Simone Weil* by Jacques Cabaud (New York: Channel Press, 1964); Richard Rees, *Simone Weil: A Sketch for a Portrait* (Carbondale: Southern Illinois University, 1966); David Anderson, *Simone Weil* (London: SCM Press, 1971); Dorothy Tuck McFarland, *Simone Weil* (New York: Ungar, 1983); John Hellman, *Simone Weil: An Introduction to Her Thought* (Philadelphia: Fortress Press, 1982); E. W. F. Tomlin, *Simone Weil* (New Haven: Yale University Press, 1954), an especially wise book whose author dares be skeptical, even show a sense of humor, in the face of certain "moments" in an astonishing, arresting life; and in French, Victor-Henry Debidour, *Simone Weil ou la transparence* (Plon, 1963).

Other books containing essays on her life which have been helpful to me are Diogenes Allen, *Three Outsiders: Pascal, Kierkegaard, Simone Weil* (Cambridge, Mass.: Cowley, 1983); *Simone Weil: Interpretations of a Life*, ed. George Abbot White (Amherst: University of Massachusetts Press, 1981); and Eric Springsted, *Affliction and the Love of God: The Spirituality of Simone Weil*, a gem of a book with an excellent bibliography (Cambridge, Mass.: Cowley, 1986). Very important, obviously, is *Simone Weil: A Bibliography*, compiled by J. P. Little (London: Grant and Cutler, 1973) and updated in 1980. That last book and Eric Springsted's will give the interested reader enough sources for a lifetime and longer of reflection.

Important critical readings can be found in the following books: William Burford's scholarly and empathic doctoral thesis on the play *Venise Sauvée*, published by University Microfilms (1967); Czeslaw Milosz's "The Importance of Simone Weil" in his *Emperor of the Earth* (Berkeley: University of California Press, 1977); Elizabeth Hardwick, "Simone Weil," such an appreciative, yet helpfully detached and ironic piece, in her *Bartleby in Manhattan* (New York: Random House, 1984); Susan Sontag, "Simone Weil" in *Against Interpretation* (New York: Farrar, Straus and Giroux, 1961), also a sympathetic but significantly critical piece; George Lichtheim's shrewd, urbane, tough yet friendly "Simone Weil" in *Collected Essays* (New York: Viking, 1973); Iris Murdoch, "On

'God' and 'Good'" in *Revisions*, ed. S. Heuerwas and A. MacIntyre (Notre Dame, Ind.: University of Notre Dame Press, 1983); and a fascinating essay by G. Lagowski, "Simone Weil and Romantic Conservatism," *Reports on Philosophy* 5, 1981.

Ongoing study of the work of Simone Weil appears in *Cahiers: Simone Weil*, "Revue trimestrielle publiée par L'Association pour L'étude de la pensée de Simone Weil," a publication many of us who keep trying to understand her various contributions find broadening, to say the least. There is, too, an American Weil Society with links to the French association; Professor Eric Springsted is the president (c/o American Weil Society, Illinois College, Jacksonville, Illinois 62650). The American Society holds yearly meetings and publishes a newsletter with important bibliographical and scholarly information, as well as copies of the papers read at an annual meeting, usually held in late April or May, with the location varying from year to year.

About the Author

Robert Coles, M.D., is professor of psychiatry and medical humanities at Harvard Medical School and research psychiatrist for the Harvard University Health Services. Among his many books are the five-volume *Children of Crisis* series, for which he was awarded the Pulitzer Prize, and works on Erik Erikson, William Carlos Williams, Walker Percy, and Flannery O'Connor. With his wife, Jane Hallowell Coles, he wrote the two volumes of *Women of Crisis*, also in the Radcliffe Biography Series. A recipient of a MacArthur Fellowship, he is continuing the research he wrote about in the much-acclaimed works *The Moral Life of Children* and *The Political Life of Children*. Dr. Coles lives near Boston with his wife and three sons.

———

Grateful acknowledgment is made to the following for permission to reprint previously published material:

THE PUTNAM PUBLISHING GROUP for:

Excerpts from *Waiting on God* by Simone Weil, translated by Emma Craufurd, © 1951, G. P. Putnam's Sons, originally published as *L'Attente de Dieu* by La Colombe, Editions du Vieux Colombier, 1950.

Excerpts from *Gravity and Grace* by Simone Weil, translated by Emma Craufurd, © 1952, G. P. Putnam's Sons. Originally published as *La Pesanteur et la Grace* by Librairie Plon, 1957.

Excerpts from *The Need for Roots: Prelude to a Declaration of Duties Towards Mankind* by Simone Weil, with a Preface by T. S. Eliot, translated by A. F. Wills, © 1952, G. P. Putnam's Sons. Originally published as *L'Enracinement: Prelude à une declaration des devoirs envers l'être humain,* by Gallimard, 1949.

UNIVERSITY OF MASSACHUSETTS PRESS for excerpts from *Oppression and Liberty* by Simone Weil, © 1958 by Routledge and Kegan Paul.

PANTHEON BOOKS, a division of Random House, Inc., for excerpts from *Simone Weil: A Life* by Simone Pétrement, translated by Raymond Rosenthal, © Random House, 1976. Originally published as *La Vie de Simone Weil* by Librairie Arthème Fayard, 1973.

OXFORD UNIVERSITY PRESS for:

Excerpts from *Simone Weil: First and Last Notebooks* translated by Richard Rees, © Richard Rees, 1970. The "New York Notebook" was first published in French as *La Connaissance Surnaturelle* by Editions Gallimard.

Excerpts from *Simone Weil: Seventy Letters*, translated and arranged by Richard Rees, © Oxford University Press, 1965. Letter to Georges Bernanos was first published by Editions Gallimard.

Index

Weil, Simone (*cont.*)
  "Is There a Marxist Doc-
    trine?," 72–74
  Letter to a Priest, 42
  The Need for Roots, 18, 30,
    38, 74–75, 102–108
  "The Needs of the Soul," 38,
    78–79
  New York notebooks, 34–
    37, 145, 149–150
  Notebooks, 110
  "Reflections Concerning the
    Causes of Liberty and So-
    cial Oppression," 90–100
    passim
  "Reflections on the Right Use
    of School Studies with a
    View to the Love of God,"
    142
  "Uprootedness," 77, 79–80,
    138
  "Uprootedness in the
    Towns," 135–136
  Waiting for God, 30, 119
Weil, Sylvie (niece), 46–47
Williams, William Carlos, 24,
  139–140, 141, 149
World War I, 6, 14
World War II, 3–4, 20, 108, 122
  declaration of, 14

Young Christian Workers' Movement, 16

179